Cambridge Elements ≡

Elements in Defence Economics
edited by
Keith Hartley
University of York

DEFENCE ECONOMICS

Achievements and Challenges

Keith Hartley
University of York

CAMBRIDGE
UNIVERSITY PRESS

CAMBRIDGE
UNIVERSITY PRESS

University Printing House, Cambridge CB2 8BS, United Kingdom

One Liberty Plaza, 20th Floor, New York, NY 10006, USA

477 Williamstown Road, Port Melbourne, VIC 3207, Australia

314–321, 3rd Floor, Plot 3, Splendor Forum, Jasola District Centre,
New Delhi – 110025, India

79 Anson Road, #06–04/06, Singapore 079906

Cambridge University Press is part of the University of Cambridge.

It furthers the University's mission by disseminating knowledge in the pursuit of
education, learning, and research at the highest international levels of excellence.

www.cambridge.org
Information on this title: www.cambridge.org/9781108814850
DOI: 10.1017/9781108887243

First published 2020

A catalogue record for this publication is available from the British Library.

ISBN 978-1-108-81485-0 Paperback
ISSN 2632-332X (online)
ISSN 2632–3311 (print)

Defence Economics

Achievements and Challenges

Elements in Defence Economics

DOI: 10.1017/9781108887243
First published online: July 2020

Keith Hartley
University of York

Author for correspondence: Keith Hartley, kh2@york.ac.uk

Abstract: This Element introduces students, policymakers, politicians, governments and business people to this new discipline within economics. It presents the recent history of the subject and its range of coverage. Traditional topics covered include models of arms races, alliances, procurement and contracting, as well as personnel policies, industrial policies and disarmament. Newer areas covered include terrorism and the economics of war and conflict. A non-technical approach is used and the material will be accessible to both economists and general readers.

Keywords: conflict economics, defence economics, disarmament, peace economics, terrorism

ISBNs: 9781108814850 (PB), 9781108887243 (OC)
ISSNs: 2632-332X (online), 2632–3311 (print)

Contents

Introduction

Defence economics is a relatively recent addition to the discipline of economics. One of the pioneering texts in the field was *The Economics of Defense in the Nuclear Age* published in 1960 (Hitch and McKean, 1960). Other pioneering developments followed in the 1960s with economic analysis applied to arms races (Richardson, 1960), the weapons acquisition process (Peck and Scherer, 1962), military alliances (Olson and Zeckhauser, 1966) and military personnel (Oi, 1967).

Another landmark in the development of the discipline came with the launch of a new academic journal, namely, *Defence Economics*, which was first published in January 1990. Publication of the journal signalled that the field of defence economics was a recognised and acceptable specialism within the academic discipline of economics. In 1994, the journal's name was changed to *Defence and Peace Economics* and later, publication expanded from four to six issues annually. The launch by Cambridge University Press of the new Elements in Defence Economics series further establishes the field within the economics discipline.

This Element focuses on the achievements of defence economics and some of the challenges it has faced. The review of achievements starts by defining defence economics, outlining a brief review of the main literature and presentation of the defence economics problem. The main fields of the subject are surveyed giving their theoretical and empirical contributions. The field has not remained static and new developments are discussed, including contributions to the economics of conflict, disarmament, peace and terrorism. The remaining challenges facing defence economics are considered, including data availability and the problems of measuring defence output.[1]

1 Achievements

Since 1960 and the publication of Hitch and McKean's *The Economics of Defense in the Nuclear Age*, much has been achieved as reflected in large numbers of theoretical and empirical publications. Defence is not static. It is characterised by change in the form of new threats and new technology. Nations are faced with ever changing threats to their national security reflected in new military alliances and coalitions. Examples include the emergence of threats from Nazi Germany and Japan, in the 1930s and early 1940s, and the later threats from the former Soviet Union, in the late 1940s, leading to the formation

---

[1] This Element presents an Overview of the discipline and it is not a detailed Review of the Literature. Such a Literature Review is available in Sandler and Hartley (1995); Hartley and Sandler (2001); and Sandler and Hartley (2007).

of new military alliances, namely, NATO and the Warsaw Pact. A new strategic environment emerged following the end of the Cold War and the abolition of the Warsaw Pact with some former members of the Pact changing membership to join NATO. Changing threats affect levels of military spending: increased threats lead to higher defence spending; reduced threats lead to disarmament. The end of the Cold War led to a more peaceful world with disarmament offering prospects of a 'peace dividend'.

Threats are not the only driver of change affecting defence. New technology brings further change and defence has been greatly affected by technical progress leading to new and costlier weapons. Guns have replaced bows and arrows; cannons meant the end of castles; tanks have replaced cavalry; aircraft and missiles emerged as new weapons; nuclear weapons have replaced some conventional forces; nuclear-powered submarines have replaced conventional battleships; and space is a new frontier for warfare. Communications have increased in importance and cyber warfare has emerged.

Such new technologies have resulted in new arms industries and the companies working within them, as well as new combat forces and even completely new armed forces (e.g. air forces). The aircraft industry did not exist in 1900. The major arms companies, such as Airbus, Boeing, BAE Systems and Lockheed Martin, did not exist before 1945 (Boeing excepted). Defence electronics has developed rapidly leading to new electronics, computer and IT industries. New technology is costly and affects defence spending and increases the importance of economics in defence policy. Armed forces and defence departments cannot ignore the costs and efficiency of their limited resources and the size of their defence budgets reflected in the 'defence economics problem'.

1.1 Definitions: Defence and Peace Economics

Various definitions are available, some reflecting the difference between defence economics and peace economics. A starting point is defence economics defined as the economics of war and peace, which can be expanded to the economics of defence, conflict, disarmament and peace. More formally, defence economics applies economic analysis to the defence economy comprising the armed forces and defence industries. As an economic problem, the focus is on choices, the alternative-use value of resources (opportunity costs) and optimising behaviour seeking to achieve an efficient allocation of resources.

Defence economists and peace economists have different viewpoints. Peace economists focus on conflict management, reduction or resolution and apply economics to understanding the causes of violent conflict and the methods by which conflict can be avoided, managed and resolved. Peace economists ana- lyse peace and quantify its value by estimating the economic cost of violence and showing that peace is a positive, tangible and achievable measure of human well-being and development. Peace economics encompasses studies of war, arms rivalry, arms control, proliferation, offence–defence balance, game theory and experimental economics. Peace economists often have a normative element in their analysis in the form of a commitment to reduce military spending and the application of economics to promote peace over efficiency in the defence economy. A recent development has been the emergence of conflict economics, which applies economic principles and methods to the study of war, terrorism, genocide, mass atrocities and peace. Conflict economics analyses these events as the result of choices that respond to incentives (Anderton and Carter, 2019).

In contrast, defence economists are more focused on positive economics and the efficiency with which the defence economy uses its resources (Anderton and Carter, 2007; Isard, 1994). Nonetheless, there are substantial overlaps between the two fields of study. Both are concerned with theoretical and empirical work on conflict, arms rivalry and arms control, arms industries, the arms trade, disarmament and the conversion of resources from military to civilian uses. Both seek reputable data sources and apply economic theory, including game theory and experimental economics methods. Contrary to popular views about security and secrecy, there are available substantial published data for defence and peace economists. The next section presents an overview of some of the major data sources. It is illustrative rather than comprehensive.

1.2 Data: Sources

Data are available from national defence ministries and departments, from government and international agencies (e.g. the US Congress, UK Parliament, United Nations (UN), NATO, European Union (EU)) and from 'think tanks' such as the Stockholm International Peace Research Institute (SIPRI), the International Institute for Strategic Studies (IISS), the Rand Corporation and the Correlates of War Project.

Some national defence departments publish data on military spending with varying degrees of detail. Examples of countries publishing detailed time- series data on total defence spending and their armed forces include Canada, New Zealand, the UK and the USA. Some nations also provide detailed analysis of major defence projects (e.g. the UK House of Commons Defence Committee Reports, UK National Audit Office, US Congressional Budget Office (CBO)). The US CBO provides detailed reports on various aspects of

US defence policy and spending. Examples include the financial implications of future defence spending, funding overseas conflicts and the costs of replacing the US aviation fleet (CBO, 2020).

International agencies such as NATO, the EU and the European Defence Agency (EDA) also provide time-series data on military spending and military personnel. Some sources provide both total figures and figures for some individual components. For example, NATO publishes various indicators of total spending in current and constant prices and spending on equipment, personnel and infrastructure by member states (NATO, 2019). The EDA publishes annual statistics on defence expenditure and its components, numbers of military and civilian personnel, and collaborative spending by total for the EU and for each member state (EDA, 2018).

The SIPRI is an independent international institute specialising in research on conflict, armaments, arms control and disarmament. It is a major data source for various aspects of military spending. Its *Yearbook* provides annual data on military expenditure for the world and by country, data on arms production by the top 100 arms firms, annual data on international arms transfers including explanations of the sources and methods used to collect the data (SIPRI, 2018). Public databases are also available for military expenditure, arms transfers, the top 100 arms firms and multilateral peace operations.

The International Institute for Strategic Studies (IISS), a British research institute specialising in international affairs, aims to provide accurate, objective information on international strategic issues (e.g. future conflict and cyber security; non-proliferation and nuclear policy). It publishes an annual *Military Balance*, which provides an independent and comprehensive assessment of the military capabilities of many nations. There are international comparisons of defence spending and military personnel as well as data on arms orders and deliveries together with detailed country studies (IISS, 2019).

A leading world think tank is the US Rand Corporation created in 1948 to undertake analysis and research for the US armed forces, especially for the US Air Force (USAF). Later it expanded to other areas of social science, including health care and social policy. It publishes original analysis of aspects of defence policy, including procurement options, defence industries, human capital and privatisation with supporting data (e.g. on aircraft unit costs (Rand, 2018)). Rand pioneered research in game theory and war gaming and has been associated with leading economists (e.g. Arrow; Nash; Schelling; von Neumann; Williamson).

The Correlates of War Project publishes time-series data on various types of wars (from 1816) as well as data on military expenditure, numbers of military personnel, alliances and national military capabilities (COW, 2020). Mention must also be made of a major and original data source on defence equipment costs, the *Source Book of Defence Equipment Costs* (Pugh, 2007). The *Source Book* provides data on unit production costs and cost increases for a complete range of air, land and sea systems. Examples include aircraft carriers, submarines, surface warships, tanks and artillery, fixed wing aircraft and helicopters, as well as cruise and ballistic missiles.

It should to be recognised that definitions of what constitutes defence spending vary between data sources. Some organisations publish data based on standard definitions of military expenditure. NATO data, for example, uses an agreed definition of defence expenditure and SIPRI also uses a published and standard definition of military expenditure. Some of these definitions differ from national definitions. Typically, definitions of defence spending differ due to the inclusion of 'other military forces' (e.g. national police forces), pension payments, mixed civil–military activities, peacekeeping forces and humanitarian operations. Also, some defence spending might be included in the expenditure of other government departmental and not just that of defence departments. Examples include civil defence, transport, government support for industry and R&D. Many of the examples used in this Element are taken from the UK, which is a world military power, and provides a different perspective from the US-dominated empirical literature.

1.3 Data: Stylised Facts

Examples of typical questions asked about defence include the following.

i) How do we measure a nation's defence spending and its defence burden?
ii) How much does the world spend on defence and how large are its military forces?
iii) What have been the trends over time for military spending?
iv) Which are the world's top military spending nations?
v) Which nations are the largest arms exporters and importers?
vi) Which are the world's largest arms companies?
vii) Are data available on the numbers of military personnel and who has the largest army, navy and air force?
viii) How much is spent on defence R&D and which nations spend the most on military R&D?
ix) Are there measures of conflict and terrorism?
x) What are the outputs of defence spending?

Table 1.1 Illustrative data on defence spending

Topic	Answer
World's leading defence spending nation: 2018	USA: US$649.0 billion; US defence share of GDP: 3.2%
World defence spending: 2018	$1,780 billion
World defence spending trends over time (constant 2017 prices)	1990: US$1,411 billion 2018: US$1,780 billion
Largest arms exporter: 2018	USA: US$10,508 million
Largest arms importer: 2018	Saudi Arabia: US$3,810 million
Largest arms company: 2018	Lockheed Martin (USA): US$47,260 million of annual arms sales
Numbers of world military personnel: 2017	27.5 million
Numbers of military personnel for European States: 2017	Land forces: 673,000 Air forces: 230,000 Naval forces: 177,000
US defence R&D spending: 2017	US$47.2 billion
Boeing (defence and aerospace) R&D: 2017	US$4.6 billion
European Union defence R&D spending, 2017)	US$1.9 billion
Terrorism and conflict	Measured by Correlates of War data; Global Terrorism Index; Global Peace Index; and ITERATE
Outputs of defence spending	Traditionally assumed that inputs equal outputs

Sources: SIPRI (2019), NATO (2019), IISS (2019), IEP (2018a, 2018b), ITERATE (2019).

Often, non-specialists believe that data are not available to answer these questions. For example, it is claimed that defence is dominated by secrecy, which makes research in the field difficult and impossible. In fact, the reality is that data are available to answer these questions. Table 1.1 presents some answers to the ten questions posed above. It can be seen that the USA is dominant in levels of defence spending, arms exports and defence R&D, and is home to the largest arms firm. By 2017, China was listed as the world's second largest arms producing nation behind the USA, with Russia in third. The largest Chinese arms company was AVIC (Aviation Industry Corporation), which was ranked sixth in the world. The Chinese North Industries Corporation (NORINCO) was ranked eighth in the world and the world's largest producer of land systems (SIPRI, 2020).[2]

Data are also available on terrorism and peace. For example, the data show a peak of deaths caused by terrorism in 2014 and a decline in deaths caused by terrorism between 2014 and 2018. The economic cost of terrorism was estimated to be US$52 billion in 2017 and US$33 billion in 2018. More widely, the economic impact of violence was estimated to be US$14.1 trillion in 2018 (IEP, 2019a, 2019b).

Table 1.1 is meant to be illustrative and not comprehensive. For example, there are questions about a nation's defence burden. There are at least two measures of burden, namely, the level of defence spending and the defence share of gross domestic product (GDP). Using defence shares of GDP shows substantial differences in defence burdens. For example, defence shares of GDP in 2018 ranged from 8.8% for Saudi Arabia and 5.3% for Algeria compared with shares of 0.4% for Ghana and 0.2% for Mauritius. Questions arise about explanations for such differences leading defence economists to develop and test models of the determinants of military spending.

Data on military spending and defence shares for the world's top fifteen nations in 2018 are presented in Table 1.2. The USA and China dominate the major spending nations. The rankings change with different measures. Based on defence shares, Saudi Arabia is a top nation together with Russia followed by the USA.

Terrorism is a relatively new form of conflict but it has a long historical tradition. In its recent form, terrorism has become international with a greater use of suicide methods. A number of data sets have emerged on transnational terrorism. One example is ITERATE, which provides data for the period 1968 to 2016 on the characteristics of transnational terrorist groups, their activities and the environment in which they operate. Inevitably, ITERATE makes judgements on the definition of terrorism. For instance, it excludes declared wars and guerrilla attacks on military targets.

Questions also arise about the determinants of a nation's defence spending and whether there are economic models of military spending, wars and conflicts. Similarly, does economic analysis contribute to an understanding of terrorism and offer any guidance on appropriate policy measures? Other topics addressed by defence and peace economics include civil wars, genocides and mass atrocities. Initial answers showing the contribution of defence economics are available by reviewing the existing literature.

---

[2] SIPRI published new data on the Chinese arms industry in January 2020 (SIPRI, 2020). These data are summarised in the text.

Table 1.2 World's top fifteen defence spending nations in 2018

Nation	Military spending (US$ billion)	Defence share of GDP (%)
USA	649.0	3.2
China	250.0	1.9
Saudi Arabia	67.6	8.8
India	66.5	2.4
France	63.8	2.3
Russia	61.4	3.9
UK	50.0	1.8
Germany	49.5	1.2
Japan	46.6	0.9
S Korea	43.1	2.6
Italy	27.8	1.3
Brazil	27.8	1.5
Australia	26.7	1.9
Canada	21.6	1.3
Turkey	19.0	2.5

Note: Countries ranked by levels of military spending.
Source: SIPRI (2019).

1.4 Brief Literature Review: Some Original Contributions

The early economists debated the 'proper' role of government. Adam Smith favoured free market capitalism but recognised a limited role for government in the form of national defence to protect the property of its citizens from theft by foreign powers. He argued that the first duty of a sovereign is the protection of society from violence and invasion by other nations. He also accepted further roles for government in the administration of justice (law and order, e.g. the enforcement of property rights and contracts), the provision of public works (e.g. transport infrastructure) and the provision of universal education (Smith, 1776). Other early economists, such as Mill, allowed a role for government in the protection of people and property and also explored the idea of soldiers as 'unproductive' labourers involved in 'useless and destructive wars' that were a 'waste of resources'. Furthermore, Mill advised on the wisdom of state intervention: '. . . interference must work for ill, if government, not understanding the subject which it meddles with, meddles to bring about a result which would be mischievous' (Mill, 1883, p. 552). Later, Alfred Marshall, reviewing the First World War, stressed the need for the public control and management of some 'crucial' industries. However, the early economists devoted little effort to the specific and specialised study of defence. This changed in 1960 with the publication of *The Economics of Defense in the Nuclear Age*.

Defence economics is a relatively new subject area within the discipline of economics. By 2020, it will be sixty years since the publication of Hitch and McKean's pioneering text book (Hitch and McKean, 1960). The publication, in January 1990, of the first academic journal, *Defence Economics*, signalled that defence economics was a recognised and accepted specialism within the academic discipline of economics. In 1994, the journal's name was changed to *Defence and Peace Economics*, emphasising its interests in peace and conflict resolution. The remainder of this section presents a limited literature review, focusing on some of the key and original contributions to the literature, all of which were published by American economists in the 1960s.

1.4.1 Economics and Defence Policy

Hitch and McKean's original and pioneering contribution applied economic analysis to defence policy and choices. It focused on efficiency in the allocation and use of defence resources and looked at military problems from an economic standpoint. On this basis, the book examines the resources available for defence and the efficiency with which defence resources are used. It starts by stressing that resources used for defence are affected by alternative uses. For example, any size of defence budget involves the sacrifice of civilian alternatives such as hospitals, schools, roads, social welfare payments or lower personal taxation. Specific weapons programmes such as a new combat aircraft or a new aircraft carrier require similar sacrifices.

The task for military commanders is to organise their limited resources to achieve specific tasks at minimum cost. Budgets measured in money costs and market prices are used to represent resource costs and the alternatives that are sacrificed by spending on defence choices. Money costs show the possibilities for substitution both *within* defence budgets and *between* defence and civil goods and services. Spending on 100 combat aircraft at US$100 million per plane means a sacrifice of, say, five aircraft carriers or 2,000 tanks. These are simplistic examples since they exclude the costs of other inputs, such as military personnel, support and maintenance. Similarly, a defence budget of US$50 billion means a sacrifice of, say, fifty schools or twenty-five hospitals. In democracies, actual choices about the size of the defence budget and its allocation between air, land and sea forces are made by politicians (elected by voters) and by military commanders (appointed by government).

Inevitably, the economic approach to defence choices encountered opposition from established interest groups. Military commanders will claim that defence budgets should be based on their assessment of defence needs and this is reflected in their use of language. Words like 'essential, vital, indispensable and the absolute minimum' will dominate debates about defence budgets. Often, we are told by the military that we 'must have' a fifty warship navy or an air force of 500 combat aircraft or an army of 100,000 soldiers (the numbers are illustrative). Economists are not popular with the military when they confront such claims by requesting information on their costs. What are the costs of a specific defence need? Is it vital regardless of costs and what would you as a military commander sacrifice to achieve your vital, essential and indispensable needs? There is a further question, namely, what are the contribution of such vital, essential and indispensable needs to defence output and what would be the impact on defence output of small, incremental or marginal changes in spending on specific weapons programmes or military forces?

These basic economic ideas and questions were not remote abstract concepts. Instead, they had a revolutionary impact on defence policy, planning, budgeting and project appraisal. Charles Hitch became Assistant Secretary of Defense (1961–5), in the US Department of Defense under Defense Secretary Robert McNamara, where he was able to apply his economic ideas to defence. He made a major contribution with the introduction of a new budgetary system known as the Planning, Programming and Budgeting System (PPBS: see below). This represented a move from input to output budgeting. Traditionally, defence budgets focused on inputs in the form of military personnel costs, procurement, R&D, operations, maintenance and construction. Output budgeting focused on the missions, final products or objectives of the armed forces, such as strategic nuclear forces, conventional land, sea and air forces, special forces, transport forces and R&D with annual costs presented for each mission.

PPBS also involved the appraisal of specific projects and military capabilities using cost-effectiveness analysis. This requires the identification of the costs and effectiveness of alternative weapons and military forces in achieving a specific objective. For example, the air defence of a city can be achieved by manned fighter aircraft or ground-based missiles and these alternatives need to be assessed in relation to their costs and effectiveness. But problems remain in the form of measuring defence output. Budgets show military capabilities (such as the numbers of warships, submarines, combat aircraft, transport aircraft and numbers of infantry soldiers, tank squadrons and artillery regiments), however, numbers do not indicate the value of these defence forces. Moreover, by themselves, numbers do not show performance in relation to potential enemy force. Nor does effectiveness 'solve' the problem since no measures of monetary value of, say, air defence are available (Hartley, 2018). Similarly, quantification is not always the answer. Performance measures in the form of numbers of bombs dropped or combat missions flown or kill-ratios can be misleading. In the Vietnam War, bombs dropped and kill-ratios led to conclusions that the Viet Cong were defeated; but they kept appearing and fighting effectively and successfully!

Misunderstandings arise when economic analysis is applied to military choices. Economically efficient solutions do not mean a cheaper force or a smaller defence budget. Economics simply provides a way of looking at military choices. Nor does economic analysis mean buying cheap or obsolescent equipment. As in private competitive industries, it might be more efficient to buy more expensive equipment to replace old or cheap equipment. Assessing military choices provides opportunities for applying a variety of economic techniques. These include production possibility boundaries (weapons versus schools), indifference curves (terrorism versus peaceful activities) and isoquants (substitution between nuclear and conventional forces (Hitch and McKean, 1960, ch. 7)).

1.4.2 Weapons Acquisition Policy

The 1960s saw further pioneering contributions applying economics to defence policy. These included weapons acquisition, military alliances and the draft. A pioneering study of the weapons acquisition process was published by Peck and Scherer (1962) with a companion volume by Scherer (1964). Peck and Scherer applied economic analysis to the acquisition of advanced weapons using historical case studies of twelve weapon systems programmes compared with seven commercial products. There is a focus on uncertainty during the development phase of advanced weapons and the implications for cost overruns, delays and project performance. Uncertainty and the dominance of government as a monopsony customer preclude a market in weapons. Peck and Scherer provide a detailed account of the structure and dynamics of the weapons industry with data on costs and profits. The companion volume by Scherer (1964) deals with competition and contractual incentives in weapons acquisition and alternative government policies for improved incentives. Different types of arms contracts are analysed embracing cost-plus, fixed price and incentive types. However, Scherer admits serious reservations about the morality of contemporary weapons development and production efforts and the focus on the efficiency of the weapons acquisition process (Scherer, 1964, p. ix).

1.4.3 Alliances

Military alliances, such as NATO, have also been analysed by economists. As a military alliance NATO is controversial and topical. It survived the end of the Cold War and its membership has expanded with former adversaries becoming new members (e.g. Hungary and Poland). It has adjusted to new military technologies and changing threats and no member state has exited the alliance. But burden-sharing debates have recurred throughout the history of the alliance, especially the continued complaint that the USA bears a disproportionate burden with European nations 'free riding' on US defence efforts. The economic theory of alliances addressed some of these issues (Olson and Zeckhauser, 1966).

NATO is a voluntary international club that specialises in supplying a single product in the form of collective defence. Collective defence has specific public good characteristics and nations will join NATO and remain members so long as membership is worthwhile. Benefits of membership take the form of collective defence including the protection offered by the US strategic nuclear umbrella and the commitment of members whereby an attack on one member is regarded as an attack on all members. Economic models of alliances view collective defence in the form of deterrence as a pure public good characterised by non-rivalry and non-excludability. The US strategic nuclear umbrella can protect additional members of the club without reducing the protection available to existing members (non-rivalry). And once deterrence is provided, it is available to everyone: exclusion is costly and not worthwhile (non-excludability). These characteristics of collective defence as a public good provide incentives to 'free ride' within an alliance.

The original version of the alliance model offered predictions on burden sharing. The most famous was the exploitation hypothesis whereby large rich allies will bear the defence burden for smaller and poorer allies. Unequal burden sharing leads to a free rider problem where some nations rely on the provision of defence by their allies. Initially, evidence supported the exploitation hypothesis with the large allies carrying the defence burdens of the smaller allies. However, military alliances have to adjust to change, including new technology (e.g. cruise missiles), new strategic doctrines (end of Cold War; flexible response) and new threats (terrorism).

1.4.4 Draft and Voluntary Recruitment

Another original contribution to knowledge was made by economic studies of military personnel, specifically the issue of recruiting personnel through a draft (conscription) or by relying on voluntary recruitment. In the 1960s, most nations relied on conscription for obtaining military manpower for their armed forces. Conscription was a form of compulsory servitude where a nation's citizens, usually young males, were required to serve in the armed forces for a minimum period of time (e.g. two years in the UK). Conscription or national service was abolished in the UK in 1960 with an all-volunteer force (AVF) achieved by 1963 and in the USA an AVF was created in 1973. Over the period 1967 to 1973, US economists were actively involved in the debate about the draft and the AVF. In the USA, President Nixon established the Gates Commission to report on an All-Volunteer Armed Force (Gates, 1970). The context was the Vietnam War with its major draft demands, criticism of the selection procedures (e.g. criteria for exemptions) and a concern about discrimination against low income, less educated and under-privileged members of society. Critics of the draft pointed to social unrest, public protests and its economic impacts in the form of labour market choices encouraging students to remain in education (adding to college recruitment), to flee to other countries (e.g. Canada), to take other actions to avoid the draft and its impact on career and life-time choices (e.g. marriage; partnerships). US conscription was seen as a selective and discriminatory tax, which led to the reduced combat effectiveness of US military manpower in Vietnam. Overall, the US draft was viewed as inequitable. Those drafted placed their lives at risk, received a fraction of pay in the civilian labour market, all for tasks they did not want to do while others could escape that responsibility. One member of the Gates Commission was the economist Professor Milton Friedman, who was an active opponent of the draft. In February 1970, the Gates Commission reported and recommended that the military draft be abolished and replaced by an AVF supported by an effective standby draft.

The debate about the draft versus an AVF meant that economists addressed a relatively neglected, but major, part of the military budget, namely, military personnel issues. The draft raised efficiency issues, which were readily addressed using economic analysis. Economists viewed the draft in terms of the price of labour relative to the price of capital or equipment (weapons). Labour and capital or weapons are factor inputs for producing defence output with possibilities of substitution between these factor inputs. The draft provided cheap labour, which was paid less than its market value and so encouraged military commanders to adopt labour-intensive military forces. Conscription also required a major military training industry but the armed forces 'lost' their valuable investments in human capital after compulsory military service. Replacing the draft by an AVF immediately increases the price of labour making it more expensive relative to the price of equipment. Economic theory predicts that a higher price for labour will lead to substitution effects with equipment or weapons replacing costlier labour: the result will be lower employment and more equipment.[3] Further substitution effects will occur between skilled and unskilled labour, between reserves and regulars, between military personnel and civilians and between men and women (Hartley, 2011, ch. 13; Oi, 1967).

Debates about the relative benefits and costs of the draft versus an AVF are a good example of applied economics in the form of economic theory, quantitative analysis and policy evaluation. In addition to substitution effects, an AVF was expected to lead to greater motivation and increased productivity, more re-enlistments with lower labour turnover and reduced training costs. There were also questions about the budget costs of adopting an AVF. For the USA, the 1970 Gates Commission Report estimated that an AVF would involve an additional annual budget cost of $2.1 billion (1970 prices: Bicklser et al., 2004).

1.5 Economics, Efficiency and Defence

Efficiency is a central focus of economics. It has a specific meaning and requires certain conditions to be implemented. Economic efficiency is about society's use of scarce resources. An economically efficient outcome occurs when it is impossible to reallocate resources to make someone better off without making someone else worse off. This is *allocative efficiency* which requires society to choose its socially desirable or 'best' output. *Technical efficiency* requires the use of the least-cost methods to produce society's preferred output. Economic theory addresses economic efficiency by using an abstract notion of a social welfare function showing society's preferences between civil goods and services and security as provided by defence spending.[4] Choices between butter and guns are limited by society's total resources: more defence means less butter (civil goods and services). This is an immediate lesson for defence planners, namely, that defence choices are limited by resource scarcity. Where resources are scarce, choosing one thing requires the sacrifice of something else (the economist's opportunity costs).

Economic models show that in private enterprise economies, an efficient allocation of resources is achieved in competitive markets. This raises questions

---

[3] Technically, economists analyse the problem by applying iso-quants and budget constraints in the form of relative factor prices. Iso-quants show various levels of defence output and budget constraints show what can be bought with a given budget and given relative factor prices for labour and capital (weapons).

[4] Reality means that social welfare functions are restricted to the realm of economic theory. No one has ever seen such a function and it is not known how it would be obtained. For example, majority voting systems are unable to obtain a clear ranking of society's choices needed to construct a social welfare function (c.f. the UK's debate about Brexit and interpretation of the Referendum result).

about the definition of defence markets and how far defence markets resemble the competitive model?

1.6 Defence Markets

In principle, defence markets allow mutually advantageous trade and exchange. They bring together buyers and sellers of various factor inputs, goods and services all of which are required to produce defence output. There is not a single defence market but, in reality, a variety of sub-markets. Some are highly specialised focusing on trading in lethal equipment, such as combat aircraft, missiles, tanks, submarines and warships. Lethal equipment is bought by national governments resulting in one or a few buyers (including arms exports) and a few suppliers or even a monopoly supplier. Other sub-markets are not specialised and trade in goods and services which are generally available in civil markets with large numbers of buyers and sellers. Examples include motor cars, computers, mobile phones and housing where such products exist and can be bought off-the-shelf. Services are also required and these can be provided 'in-house' by the armed forces or outsourced to private suppliers. Outsourcing involves state finance and private provision with government paying for the services but private industry providing the service. Examples of outsourcing include repair and maintenance work, catering and cleaning, aircrew training, the management of military bases and the supply of air tankers (Hartley, 2011, ch. 14).

1.6.1 Military Personnel

Labour markets are a further sub-market within defence markets. Armed forces require large numbers of military personnel with requirements ranging from unskilled labour to skilled labour. Armed forces are not the only buyers of labour and they have to compete with large numbers of civilian employers demanding personnel. This means that military personnel have to be paid at least the average wage rate in the civilian sector plus an addition to reflect the net disadvantages of military service. Disadvantages include military discipline, hours of work, overseas service, and the possibility of injury and death in service (e.g. conflict). As a result, the military employment contract is unique. Military personnel are subject to military law and discipline; they have to obey orders; they are liable to be deployed to any area of the world at short notice and for indefinite periods; they might operate in hazardous conditions working for long hours; and they might be injured or killed. The contract specifies length of service and establishes ownership rights in military personnel: in some respects it resembles a contract of slavery.

Typically, the armed forces provide training for their recruits in general and specific skills. General training has market value in the civilian economy and includes computer skills, some pilot training, driving skills as well as security, mercenary and policing skills. Specific training has value to the military only and examples include combat aircraft pilots, tank gunners, submariners and missile operatives. For specialist military skills, the national defence ministry is a monopsony buyer (e.g. combat aircraft pilots; tank drivers; nuclear submarine captains). Training costs are usually borne by the armed forces and the forces obtain a return on their training investments reflected in the duration of the military employment contract. Costly training usually requires long-service contracts to enable the military to obtain a return on its training investments (e.g. combat aircraft pilots).

1.7 Market Failure

Defence markets usually fail to resemble the competitive model for some very good reasons. Market failure arises from the public goods features of defence markets, from specific features of the buying and supply sides of the market and from the lack of incentive and penalty mechanisms in some defence markets.

1.7.1 Public Goods

Defence and peace are regarded as classic examples of public goods. Public goods differ from private goods, which are bought by consumers in markets. For private good such as motor cars, personal computers and restaurant meals, consumption benefits are restricted to each individual and are at the expense of other individuals. In contrast, public goods are non-rival and non-excludable. For example, one citizen's consumption of nuclear deterrence does not affect another citizen's consumption of deterrence and, once provided, other citizens cannot be excluded from consuming nuclear deterrence. The public good features of defence (and peace) provide incentives for free riding. Since citizens cannot be excluded from the benefits of defence and since there is no rivalry in consumption, people have incentives to let others pay for defence. Free riding means that citizens will fail to reveal their true preferences for, and valuation of, defence. As a result, controversies arise both within nations and between nations in a military alliance. Examples include NATO burden-sharing debates between the USA and Europe and similar disputes between the USA and Canada with Canada free riding on US defence spending. Economic theory offers theoretical solutions to the problem of estimating the optimal amount of a public good such as defence but such solutions are difficult to operationalise and implement in practice (Sandler, 1992).[5]

In addition to public goods, there are other sources of failure in defence markets. Competitive markets are characterised by large numbers of buyers and sellers, both of which are generally absent in defence markets. Instead, the buying side of defence markets, especially for specialised weapons, is dominated by government often acting as a major, sole or single buyer (monopsony). For example, a national government is usually the sole buyer of nuclear weapons, nuclear-powered submarines and inter-continental ballistic missiles (ICBMs). Defence markets do not have the large numbers of buyers that characterise competitive markets. Instead, government as a major or single buyer of lethal equipment can use its buying power to determine the size, structure, conduct, performance and ownership of its national defence or arms industry. Rearmament and wars increase the demand for military equipment while peace leads to disarmament and smaller defence industries. Similarly, military demands for new equipment have an impact on technical progress. For example, military demands especially in the First World War led to the creation of the aircraft industry and the R&D required for new aircraft. The result was new forms of propulsion, new materials, new production methods, new methods of navigation, greater speeds and longer range (Hartley, 2014).

The supply side of defence markets departs from the competitive model where there is a large number of rival suppliers each seeking maximum profits. In contrast, defence industries are imperfect with monopoly, duopoly or oligopoly suppliers (one, two or a few suppliers). Some defence industries are state-owned rather than privately owned with state ownership leading to the pursuit of non-profit objectives (e.g. employment, regional jobs) and a reluctance to adjust to change.

Furthermore, armed forces on the supply side of defence markets are public sector bureaucracies and monopoly suppliers of air, land and sea forces with monopoly property rights in each domain. Monopoly power and property rights within the armed forces means that there are barriers to new entry preventing rival armed forces from offering new and competing products. Consider, for example, the problems faced by the army when seeking to provide ground-based missile defences to replace manned combat aircraft operated by the air force; or the air force offering to replace aircraft carriers with land-based aircraft

---

[5] More generally, these are collective or group action problems where the supply of some goods requires the co-ordination of actions and efforts by two or more individuals. Examples include groups such as trade unions and clubs such as golf, angling and tennis clubs. Collective action might be voluntary or state-provided. Defence is a collective action good which is not provided voluntarily but is state-provided and state-financed.

and to replace naval anti-submarine warships with air force maritime patrol aircraft; or the army using attack helicopters to replace air force close support aircraft. Private markets address these substitution possibilities between the armed forces through incentive and penalty mechanisms and through capital markets. The armed forces lack entrepreneurs seeking profits by introducing new ideas and new production methods. Military commanders are not entrepreneurs motivated by profitability. The absence of a private and competitive capital market is a further source of inefficiency within the armed forces. Such an absence means that military commanders are not rewarded for successes nor penalised for failures through job losses. Without a capital market, there are no opportunities and mechanisms for rewarding successful mergers and take-overs. For example, a regimental commander cannot merge with another regiment to exploit economies of scale and scope; nor can an army regiment acquire air force and navy transport units, where such mergers might offer cost savings and output gains (the industry equivalents of horizontal, vertical or conglomerate mergers). Overall, the relationship between inputs and outputs is expressed in the military production function.

1.8 The Military Production Function

The military production function shows the relationship between inputs and outputs relating all defence inputs to final defence output. Inputs consist of technology, capital and labour. Technology results from defence R&D. Capital includes equipment, military bases, spare parts and infrastructure. Labour comprises military personnel in the form of volunteers and/or conscripts together with reservists, civilians employed by the military as well as contractors undertaking work for the armed forces (e.g. repair, maintenance, training, transport, management). The military production function can be expressed formally as:

$$Q = f (A, K, L)$$

where Q is defence output and A, K and L are inputs with A representing technology, K capital and L labour. The form of the relationship between the inputs and output is expressed by 'f', which in this model is a positive relationship (e.g. greater inputs result in greater outputs).

The military production function appears to be an attractive concept but it is not problem free. There are problems on both the output and inputs sides of the model. Defence output is relatively easy to define but difficult to measure and value. Compared with, say, the car industry where output is measured by the annual production of cars and other vehicles and where the volume of output is valued based on the market price of cars. There are no similar comparators for defence output. Instead, defence output is defined broadly in terms of peace, protection and security with no single output indicator nor any means of valuing such outputs and determining society's preferred defence output (the 'optimal' defence output).

Further problems arise on the input side. It is assumed that as in competitive markets, factor inputs are combined by entrepreneurs to minimise costs. For the armed forces, this is an unrealistic assumption in view of the lack of efficiency incentives in internal defence markets where there are few rewards and penalties for achieving least-cost production methods. Instead, military commanders and their staff are rewarded for good performance as military officers using military and not economic efficiency criteria. Commanders and officers will be subject to 'soft' budget constraints and they will combine factor inputs according to rules laid down by their military service (e.g. specific numbers of ground crew for each aircraft squadron). In contrast, profit-seeking entrepreneurs will continuously search for new methods of production, for new methods of organising their production and for new products. They will search for opportunities for factor substitution, such as replacing labour with capital (new technology and new machines replacing workers). For example, traditionally, the manufacture of aircraft wings was a labour-intensive operation that has now been computerised and mechanised with one worker and a computer managing large numbers of automatic riveting machines. Similar opportunities for factor substitution exist in the armed forces. Capital replacing labour arises where combat aircraft replace labour-intensive armies; nuclear weapons replace large-scale conventional forces; and unmanned air vehicles replace land operations conducted by soldiers. Further examples of factor substitution for military forces include reserves replacing regular personnel, police and civilian personnel replacing military personnel, land-based aircraft replacing naval aircraft carriers, maritime patrol aircraft replacing naval anti-submarine frigates, land-based air defence missiles replacing manned fighter aircraft, attack helicopters replacing manned combat aircraft for close air support and cruise missiles replacing manned bomber aircraft. Military history provides some dramatic examples of factor substitution, such as cannons and gunpowder rendering castles obsolescent; rifles replacing the traditional bow and arrow; tanks replacing horse cavalry; carrier-borne aircraft replacing battleships; and satellite communications replacing pigeons and observation balloons (Brauer and Van Tuyll, 2008).

Military commanders cannot ignore opportunities for factor substitution. In some cases, defeat in conflict will force them to change and adapt to new technology and new weapons (e.g. aircraft in 1914). Or, commanders might use new technology to raise their budgets where they act as budget-maximisers.

Challenges arise where new technology and new weapons might threaten the traditional monopoly property rights of each of the armed forces. Examples include land-based air defence missiles operated by the army replacing manned fighter aircraft operated by the air force; maritime patrol aircraft operated by air the force replacing naval warships; opposition from the army and navy to the creation of an independent air force following the emergence of aircraft; and private contractors undertaking tasks traditionally performed 'in-house' by the armed forces (e.g. training; transport services). In such circumstances, various interest groups will emerge to protect the traditional position (see Public Choice analysis in subsection 1.9).

There are further problems with using military production functions. All inputs have to be identified and valued. These comprise technology, physical capital and human capital. Technology will be embodied in new equipment and new military facilities, including ground and space-based communications. Physical capital consists of military equipment, such as combat aircraft, tanks and warships, together with bases, training areas and logistics including repair and maintenance. Human capital consists of military personnel with their skills reflected in their market value together with reservists and civilians employed in military tasks. Where the military use conscripts, their pay will not reflect their market value (e.g. doctors and scientists as conscripts will be paid considerably less than their market value in the civilian sector). Overall, counting numbers (e.g. aircraft, tanks and warships) is the easy part: converting numbers into market values is considerably more difficult. For instance, how are combat aircraft and warships valued? What is the value of a single naval frigate?

1.8.1 Cost-effectiveness Analysis

Usually, economic analysis of military equipment and military forces have applied *cost-effectiveness* analysis. The absence of defence output measures and valuations mean that economic analysis cannot use cost–benefit analysis but has to be restricted to cost-effectiveness studies. These use available measures of effectiveness, such as numbers of combat aircraft missions flown, numbers of enemy aircraft destroyed or number of days at sea for warships. A cost-effectiveness study of air defence would compare the costs and effectiveness of alternative systems, such as ground-based missiles versus manned fighter aircraft, or anti-submarine capability would compare land-based maritime patrol aircraft versus naval frigates or anti-tank capability would compare manned combat aircraft versus attack helicopters versus soldier-launched missiles. Cost-effectiveness is a valuable approach that is better than relying on human subjective judgement and intuition but it still lacks a monetary value for each of the different capabilities. What values are placed on the air defence, anti-submarine and anti-tank capabilities so that comparisons can be made between each capability resulting in a ranking showing best and worst of the options? Without money values for making choices about military forces, decisions are likely to be based on arguments used by various interest groups in the military-industrial complex. Such groups will seek to influence defence spending, they will be involved in arms race debates and will be influential in the membership of military alliances. They will also lobby for and against major equipment projects, such as a new warship, a new combat aircraft programme or a new tank.

1.9 The Military-Industrial-Political Complex: A Public Choice Analysis

Since government is central to understanding defence markets, there is a need for a theory of government and political markets. Public choice models provide an economic theory of political markets comprising voters, political parties, bureaucracies and interest groups, including producer groups. Each of these agents will pursue their own self-interest. Voters will seek maximum benefits (satisfaction) from casting their votes. They will evaluate the alternative policies offered by rival political parties but such evaluation is limited by a lack of information about specialist defence topics such as the threat, nuclear weapons, NATO, and the defence value of costly arms projects, such as aircraft carriers and the F-35 aircraft. Where the collection of information is costly, producers and other interest groups with specialist knowledge will seek to influence voters and political parties. For example, defence contractors building aircraft carriers will publish 'independent' research studies showing the jobs, technology and export benefits created by such major defence projects. The opportunities for producer groups to influence policy are reinforced by the limitations of the voting system as a means of accurately identifying society's prefer-ences. Often, elections are general in which voters have to choose between a diverse set of policies involving education, health, social welfare, envir-onmental issues and foreign policy. Defence policy might be only one component of the policies offered by rival political parties and voters are not able to indicate the intensity of their preferences. Nor can voters and elections commit politicians to a specific time-table so that elected govern-ments have discretion in implementing their election promises. Nor is a referendum the solution: simple yes/no options can be misleading and fail to indicate the complexity of such apparently simple options.[6]

Economic models of politics assume that governments and political parties will be vote-maximisers with governments seeking re-election and political parties aiming to form a government. A government's policies are implemented by bureaucracies. The winning party at an election captures the entire market and forms the government. Economic models of bureaucracy start by assuming that bureaucracies are budget- or utility-maximisers (Mueller, 1989). Larger budgets enable bureaucrats to obtain larger salaries, power, prestige and on-the-job leisure. There are no incentives for bureaucrats to achieve economies in supplying their output. Indeed, the output of a defence bureaucracy (and other public bureaucracies) is not measurable so making it impossible to monitor the efficiency of their production. Instead, the output of a defence bureaucracy is measured by identifiable inputs and activities, such as numbers of military personnel, combat aircraft, missiles, tanks and warships. These military units are more easily counted than are units of protection and security.

1.9.1 Principal-agent Models

Within defence markets, bureaucracies comprise defence departments or ministries and the armed forces in the form of armies, navies and air forces. Defence bureaucracies can be viewed as monopoly suppliers of information and protection to national governments that are monopsony buyers of military forces for protection. This relationship can be analysed as a principal-agent problem. Government is the principal buying defence services from its agents in the form of defence departments and the armed forces. The challenge for principals is to devise incentive mechanisms to ensure that agents pursue the aims of the principal rather than their own objectives. Defence is full of examples of the principal-agent problem. For example, during the Second World War, senior military commanders often pursued their own objectives rather than those of their principals (e.g. the strategic bombing of Germany): it was difficult and costly to monitor and control senior and junior military commanders. The principal-agent model can be expanded more widely with voters and taxpayers as principals and governments as their agents.

---

[6] For example, the UK referendum on UK membership of the EU resulted in a majority in favour of exit; but Brexit turned out to be much more complex than indicated by a simple yes/no result. For example, did Brexit mean leave with or without a deal and what sort of deal?

1.9.2 Bureaucracies

Budget-maximising models of bureaucracy predict that bureaucracies will seek to maximise their budget subject to the constraint of covering their total costs. Self-interested officials will be motivated by goals that benefit themselves rather than their bureaus or society. As a result, defence departments and the armed forces will exaggerate the threat, under-estimate costs and offer programmes that are attractive to vote-maximising governments. On this basis, the identification and exaggeration of new threats offers the prospects of higher budgets. Examples include reports of the enemy's nuclear weapons and the missile threat and the threats from terrorism and rogue states. Also, in arguing for a new weapons project, the armed forces will under-estimate its costs (optimism bias) so as to start a new project and once started projects are difficult to stop and cancel: they attract interest groups of scientists, technologists, trade unions and residents in local areas (cities; towns) with an income interest in continuation of the project (Jackson, 1982).

1.9.3 Producer Groups

Producer groups in the form of defence contractors will also seek to influence defence policy and the award of defence contracts. Such groups will pursue their own self-interest in the form of maximum profits or sales or rents (rent-seeking). In pursuit of their objectives, producer groups will use lobbying, advertising campaigns, consultancy reports and the sponsorship of politicians. Where governments consider buying defence equipment from overseas, producer groups will stress the adverse consequences for its national defence industry through losses of jobs, high technology, spin-offs, exports and the capability for independent military action. Trade unions and professional associations with members in defence industries will also support domestic arms firms so as to protect the jobs, careers and favourable income prospects of their defence workers. For example, defence contractors and unions involved in building the UK's new submarine nuclear deterrent at Barrow-in-Furness will form a strong producer group supporting continued work on the project and their views will be expressed in local election results.

1.9.4 Rent-seeking

Success in winning a defence contract means that the government provides a prize in the form of monopoly rents: hence, the pursuit of these rents has been given the name of rent-seeking (Mueller, 1989). The funds associated with a government defence contract represent a prize that is well worth winning and doing so makes it worthwhile for firms to invest resources in bidding for contracts (other examples include government construction contracts for hospitals, roads, schools and infrastructure projects). Government defence contracts provide substantial income to the firms awarded such contracts. As a result, expected contract income will determine the willingness and ability of firms to incur costs (lobbying and advertising costs, contributions to government election campaign expenditures and the running costs of political parties) as a means of winning a defence contract (Mueller, 1989). On this basis, competition for contracts uses scarce resources and the costs of competition can exceed its benefits. In the limiting case, where no benefits are created, the costs of competition are all waste so that more competition increases social waste (Mueller, 1989).

Political markets contain other interest and pressure groups that are active in defence markets. The various interest groups will represent the potential gainers and losers from defence policy. For example, the Campaign for Nuclear Disarmament (CND), the Society of Friends and environment groups (Greens) will oppose nuclear weapons and armed conflicts. The Campaign Against the Arms Trade (CATT) will oppose arms exports. Interest groups might pursue their objectives through mass demonstrations and civil disobedience or through a take-over of a political party or through non-peaceful means (e.g. assassinations, bombings, kidnappings). Furthermore, some interest groups specialise in the independent evaluation of defence policy, which provides voters and politicians with alternative sources of information. Examples include university research centres, the SIPRI and the US Rand Corporation. The international community provides further examples of groups with an interest in defence policy. These include NATO, which will lobby its members to maintain or increase their defence spending, the United Nations, which will favour peace-making including contributions to international peacekeeping forces, national governments, which will seek to influence another nation's defence spending, and foreign arms firms seeking overseas business.

1.9.5 Predictions

Public choice models provide an analytical framework for understanding the military-industrial-political complex and its influence on defence choices and budgets. They identify various groups within the complex, namely, voters, political parties, governments, the armed forces, defence departments, defence contractors, and other pressure and interest groups. Each group has different objectives that determine their behaviour. Once the various groups are recognised it is not surprising that the simple recommendations of economists (e.g.

for more competition or more free trade) will be modified into a set of policy recommendations that bear no resemblance to the original recommendations (e.g. more competition becomes more regulation or managed competition). The models appear to be realistic but realism is no substitute for analytical rigour and empirical testing. Public choice models provide some predictions relevant to understanding defence markets. For example, it is predicted that democratic governments tend to favour producers more than consumers. Producer groups dominate since they can afford the costly investments in specialist information needed to influence government and they have the most to gain from influencing policy in their favour. Furthermore, the voters who are best informed on any policy issue are those whose incomes are directly affected by it (employees in defence firms) while they are less well-informed on issues that affect them as consumers (Downs, 1957). As a result, governments will support the national defence industry through contract awards, subsidy payments and favourable profit rates on non-competitive contracts.

Public choice models provide further predictions about the military-industrial -political complex. Vote-maximising governments seeking re-election might award defence contracts to firms in marginal constituencies or in high unem-ployment areas. Or, a military base which is regarded as 'vital' to a local community might be 'saved' from closure. Similarly, budget-maximising bureaucracies are likely to be too large and inefficient. Government departments and the armed forces are monopoly suppliers of specialist information and knowledge and they will use information to their advantage. Military personnel and civil servants are experts in their fields and they can adjust and play any games. There are incentives to hoard valuable information, including informa-tion on defence outputs and the possibilities for factor substitution.

Principal-agent models show the opportunities for 'playing games' between the armed forces and government. For example, the three armed forces (army, navy and air force) operate in a small numbers game with opportunities for collusion rather than competition when bidding for defence budget. Allocating the defence budget on the basis of rotation (known as Buggins Turn) turn' is not unknown: this year it is the navy's turn for a new aircraft carrier; next year it will be the turn of the air force after which the army will receive its new tanks.

As major interest groups, the armed forces will seek to protect their tradi-tional monopoly rights, their prestige and attractive weapons projects, which often give satisfaction to their users rather than providing security and protec-tion to society. Air force pilots enjoy flying high speed combat aircraft, admirals gain prestige from operating the latest aircraft carriers and generals prefer tanks to lorries. Possibilities of substitution that affect the traditional monopoly property rights of each of the armed forces will encounter massive opposition.

Examples include attack helicopters and surface-to-air missiles operated by the army replacing close air support aircraft operated by the air force or air force maritime patrol aircraft replacing navy frigates. Opposition to such proposals will encounter massive obstacles from established military personnel and from retired admirals, air marshals and generals.

Public choice models also provide insights into proposals to reduce defence spending. A budget-maximising defence department and the armed forces will oppose measures to reduce military spending. They will use highly emotive language to resist disarmament. There will be stress on the 'dire consequences' of defence cuts and proposals to cut a specific military capability (e.g. marines, paratroopers, combat aircraft squadrons, naval frigates and army tanks). References will be made to the continuing threat from nations such as China, Iran and Russia, as well as new and emerging threats from international terrorism and from what are believed to be failed or rogue states (e.g. Iran, North Korea, ISIS). Proposals to cancel major weapons projects will be opposed by focusing on the economic impacts in terms of losses of jobs, technology and spin-offs and lost exports. Cancellations also mean the prospect of greater dependence on foreign suppliers and the loss of independence and national security.

While producer groups are central to public choice models there is a gap in our knowledge and understanding of such groups. Often there are vague references to major defence contractors as powerful and influential pressure groups. Critics readily identify major arms firms as producer groups. On this basis, an analysis of the major arms firms and their markets can be used to identify the features of such producer groups. They are likely to be large in both absolute and relative size and to be domestic monopolies. They will be highly dependent on national defence business, they might be located in marginal constituencies or in high unemployment areas and they are likely to be awarded major defence contracts on a non-competitive basis.

Overall, public choice models embracing the economics of politics, bureaucracies and producer groups identify the agents in political markets, their behaviour and likely impact on defence policies. The analysis shows which groups will gain and which will lose from changes in defence policy and spending. However, attractive descriptions of reality are not sufficient for the acceptance of a model. More work is needed to operationalise the approach. Public choice models need to be compared with alternative models that explain defence spending and policy. The research question is whether public choice analysis provides better explanations compared with other models which ignore political markets? The next section considers the determinants of defence spending.

1.10 What Determines Military Spending?

A starting point is the standard economic theory of demand. On this basis, a demand function for military expenditure can be represented by a general equation of the following form:

$ME = f(P, Y, A, T, W, Z)$

where ME is military expenditure measured in constant prices; P is the relative price of military and civil goods and services; Y is income measured by real GDP; A is a military alliance variable measured by NATO defence spending; T represents a threat variable; W is a war variable; and Z comprises all other relevant factors (e.g. political composition of government; geo-political factors such as end of the Cold War).

Next, data are required to represent these variables. In some instances, data are unavailable, such as measures for the relative prices of military and civil goods. Sometimes, researchers proceed by ignoring relative prices or by assuming there is no relative price effect (an assumption that needs to be tested). Similar problems arise with the threat variable where one solution would be to use data on the military spending of potential enemies (e.g. military spending for China, Iran, North Korea and Russia). However, reliable data are not always available to measure the threat: published data might be inaccurate or only a partial indicator of military spending (e.g. there is a lack of a standard international definition; some items of spending might be omitted). Threats result in arms races.

1.11 Arms Races

Mention of threats leads to another specific explanation of military spending concerned with arms races. Models of an arms race show a nation's military spending reacting to the military spending of a rival nation (i.e. international competition in military spending). Nations increase military spending as a response to increases in military spending by a potential enemy nation. A simple arms race model based on military spending is represented (based on Lewis Richardson, 1960):

$dX = a_0 - a_1 X + a_2 Y$
$dY = b_0 - b_1 Y + b_2 X$

where dX, dY are the changes in military spending over time of the two nations, X and Y; a_0 and b_0 are grievance terms for each nation. Grievance could be the desire for revenge for past wrongs and defeats (e.g. Germany after the Second World War); a_1, b_1 are fatigue factors reflecting the economic burdens of military spending (e.g. guns verus butter) and their negative signs show that higher military spending involves greater economic burdens reflected in greater sacrifices of civil goods; a_2, b_2 are reaction coefficients showing the arms race effect where each nation responds to the defence spending of its rival. While this version of the arms race model is based on military spending, international rivalry could be based on specific weapons. Examples include arms races based on numbers of battleships, numbers of soldiers, numbers of overseas military bases, and numbers of nuclear weapons and missiles.

There are numerous examples of arms races that make the model appear attractive. They include the superpower arms race between the USA and former Soviet Union during the Cold War, the Middle East arms races between Israel and Arab nations, between India and Pakistan, between South American states, between Iran and Saudi Arabia and between North and South Korea. However, while the examples appear persuasive, they are not adequate empirical tests of the model. Empirical tests of arms race models have provided only limited explanations of military spending (Hartley and Sandler, 2001; Sandler and Hartley, 1995). Military alliances are another determinant of a nation's defence spending.

1.12 Military Alliances: The Impact of NATO

Economists have developed models of military alliances, such as NATO which is analysed as providing a pure public good in the form of collective defence with non-rival and non-excludable benefits. International peacekeeping forces provide a similar public good in the form of international peace which promotes international trade and exchange. The original pioneering work on the economics of alliances was undertaken by Mancur Olson and subsequently published in Olson and Zeckhauser (1966).

Economic models of military alliances, such as NATO, predict that for a member state, the more defence a nation's allies provide, the less that member tends to spend on defence (free riding). Also, because the larger members of an alliance place a higher valuation on protection and security, they will tend to allocate larger shares of their national income to defence than smaller nations (exploitation of the larger nations by the smaller nations). However, changes in NATO strategy from reliance on nuclear forces and nuclear deterrence to flexible response led to new developments in the economic models of alliances. The *joint products model* was formulated to recognise the alliance producing a variety of military outputs comprising nuclear deterrence, protection or damage limitation provided by conventional forces and nation-specific benefits also provided by conventional forces (flexible response). A variety of military outputs means that they are a mix of purely public, purely private or impurely public among allies. Conventional forces provide both deterrence and damage-limiting protection and are subject to force thinning as a given amount of conventional forces are used to defend a longer border or a larger geographical area. For example, defence spending in response to a terrorist threat confined to a member state and of no benefit to other allies yields largely private benefits to the providing nation. The UK's increased defence spending to counter the threat from the IRA in Northern Ireland was of benefit only to the UK (but provided public benefits to the population of Northern Ireland and the rest of the UK (Hartley and Sandler, 2001).

By 2019, NATO celebrated its seventieth anniversary. Over this period, it has survived many changes reflecting changing threats, new technology, new strategic security environments and new US Presidents raising the question of why it has survived. Its rival Warsaw Pact has been abandoned and former members of the Pact have joined NATO. Critics focus on unequal burden sharing between the USA and Europe with US accusations that the Europeans are 'free riding' on US defence efforts. Member states have responded with a target commitment to spend 2% of GDP on defence. Even if all members implement this target, there remain problems. The 2% target does not specify its public–private mix: member states will have incentives to focus on private goods since these produce greater national benefits.

1.13 The Benefits of Defence Spending: Growth and Prosperity

Cost–benefit analysis can be used to assess the level of a nation's defence spending. One measure of costs is presented in the annual defence budget but benefits are more difficult to identify and value. Benefits are viewed as contributions to economic growth and prosperity.

The relationship between military spending and economic growth has resulted in a considerable theoretical and empirical literature. There are two alternative hypotheses. First, that military spending favourably affects economic growth (Benoit, 1973). Second, that military spending has the opposite impact by adversely affecting a nation's growth rate (Deger and Smith, 1983; Hartley and Sandler, 2001). Immediately, questions arise about the causal relationships involved.

Consider the favourable impact hypothesis. Military spending might stimulate economies with large-scale unemployment; and there might be technology impacts and spin-offs from military spending. Growth can also be enhanced if some military spending is used to provide social infrastructure, especially in less developed countries (e.g. airports, roads, tunnels and ports). Defence spending might further contribute to growth through human capital effects (education, training discipline and motivation). Furthermore, defence spending maintains external and internal protection and security which promotes beneficial trade and exchange.

The negative impact hypothesis arises where defence diverts resources from more productive alternative civil uses. This is known as the crowding-out effect with crowding-out involving private investment, exports and R&D resources. For example, some defence R&D might not have valuable spin-offs to the civilian sector (e.g. stealth technology: who would wish to fly in a stealthy airliner?). Both the favourable and negative impact hypotheses need to be assessed critically considering also the counterfactual. For example, not all civilian R&D is successful: there are often failures. Uncertainty means that no one can predict accurately the future: it is unknown and unknowable. Overall, the net effect of defence spending on growth depends on the relative strengths of the positive and negative impacts. The issue has been the focus of myths, emotion and special pleading and has generated a massive literature with evidence supporting both positive and negative impacts!

Any assessment of these rival hypotheses needs to start from a properly specified model of economic growth. Usually, defence spending is simply added to a conventional economic model of growth without careful consideration of its causal impacts on growth. Empirical tests have often used Granger causality tests but these have their limitations (e.g. parameters may not be stable over time; they are not tests of economic causality (Dunne and Smith, 2010)). Empirical results are further affected by differences between developed and less developed countries, between different time periods and between cross-section and time-series studies. Following a review of the literature, it was concluded that 'the net impact of defence on growth is negative, but small' (Sandler and Hartley, 1995, p. 220). A more recent study concluded that debates on the economic effects of military spending continue to develop, showing the limitations of previous work but without any consensus in the literature. Adjusting for endogeneity in defence-growth relationships found that the negative and damaging impacts of military spending on growth have been significantly underestimated in most studies (d'Agostino et al., 2019; Matthews, 2019).

Further benefits from defence spending arise through its contribution to national prosperity. This contribution takes two forms. First, defence spending provides protection from external attack, which allows a nation's citizens to pursue peaceful trade and exchange. A further related benefit includes the protection of international trade routes (air and sea routes), which promote global trading opportunities and provide a public good. Second, within an economy, defence provides wider economic benefits in the form of national output (GDP), jobs, technology and exports. Some of these wider economic benefits can be measured but there is no single indicator that aggregates different indicators (e.g. aggregation of employment numbers and export sales plus number of patents), nor are there any money values for these performance indicators. Alternatives cannot be ignored. Alternative spending creates jobs and contributes to technology and spin-offs as well as exports and import-savings. Questions then arise about the comparative contribution of defence spending versus alternative expenditures. Does defence spending make a greater contribution to jobs, compared to spending on hospitals, houses, roads and schools?

In addressing the prosperity contribution of defence spending, basic questions arise about the definition of prosperity: what is it? Protection and security relate to economic measures of welfare, such as per capita income, but prosperity embraces much more aspects of the quality of life such as freedoms of speech and movement and other aspects of liberty (e.g. free press, television and broadcasting, democratic values and democracy). Economists have a long tradition of efforts to measure individual utility and satisfaction reflected in debates about cardinal and ordinal utilities. Immediately, problems arise in measuring utility and in making inter-personal comparisons of utility. For society as a whole, concepts of social welfare have been formulated but no one has ever seen a social welfare function for, say, the UK and USA showing the trade-offs between guns and butter. Whatever the views on defence and prosperity, continued rising costs are a major challenge for defence policymakers.

1.14 Rising Costs: A Challenge

Defence equipment is costly and costs have continued rising. Norman Augustine showed '. . . that the unit cost of certain high technology hardware is increasing at an exponential rate with time' (Augustine, 1987, p. 140). Since the start of the aviation age, the unit cost of tactical aircraft has increased by a factor of four every ten years. Similar trends apply to civil aircraft and helicopters; but for ships and tanks, unit cost growth has been much lower at a factor of two every ten years. Comparisons of unit cost growth with national defence budget growth led Augustine to predict that by the year 2054, the entire US defence budget would only buy one aircraft. The aircraft would be available for the air force and navy 3.5 days each week and in leap years it would be available to the marines for the extra day. This was known as Augustine's First Law of Impending Doom or the Final Law of Economic Disarmament (Augustine, 1987, p. 143). These forecasts apply to all nations although the dates will differ. For example, the UK with a considerably smaller defence budget will reach the 2054 position two years earlier than the USA.

1.14.1 Cost Escalation

The Augustine Laws have generated further studies of rising unit costs. Kirkpatrick and Pugh (1983) confirmed rising real unit costs of UK defence equipment with the unit costs of combat aircraft rising at an average rate of about 8% per year. Such rising costs have led to forecasts of a single tank army, single warship navy and a *Starship Enterprise* representing the air force. Further estimates show UK real annual unit cost growth between 1955 and 2011 ranging from 2.6% for destroyers to almost 6% for combat aircraft and main battle tanks (Davies et al., 2011). Unit cost growth is defined specifically and differs from *defence inflation*, which measures the annual change in the cost of defence goods and services of a given type and quality. In contrast, unit cost growth refers to the increased costs associated with moving from one generation of equipment to the next generation. For example, the unit costs of Tornado compared with the next generation Typhoon combat aircraft. Such cost increases are known as *intergenerational equipment cost growth or cost escalation* and are usually presented in constant prices or real terms (Davies et al., 2011). However, different studies use different definitions of unit costs and different time periods. Some refer specifically to unit production costs while others refer to unit costs, which presumably includes both development and production costs, with estimates presented in real or money terms (the distinction is not always clear). Furthermore, some studies use unit costs data adjusted for equipment performance: for example, warship unit costs might be in terms of unit costs per ton of weight.

The causes of cost escalation have been addressed. Interestingly, the first observation is that technical progress in the civil economy usually leads to reductions in unit costs and prices, but not for defence equipment. One explanation of cost escalation is that defence equipment is a 'tournament good'. Military superiority requires that a nation's equipment is technically superior to that of its potential rival or enemy. However, achieving technical superiority is costly. Other explanations for cost escalation include the inefficiencies of national monopoly defence industries, which are usually protected from foreign competition (Davies et al., 2011). Or, agents in the military-industrial-political complex are prone to 'optimism bias': they always expect defence equipment to be delivered on time and at the originally estimated cost. A US study estimated that about one-third of aircraft cost escalation was due to economy factors (e.g. economy-wide price trends in labour, equipment and materials) and two-thirds was due to customer-driven factors (e.g. greater aircraft stealth, reduced aircraft weight) (Arena et al. 2008; Hartley, 2020).

Unit cost growth has major economic effects on the armed forces and defence industries. Rising unit costs and defence budgets that do not increase as rapidly mean that the armed forces have to reduce their equipment numbers with fewer being bought of a given type. The result is smaller numbers of aircraft for the air force, fewer warships for the navy and fewer tanks for the army. Smaller quantities being bought means smaller production runs for defence industries and a reduction in scale and learning economies. Rising development costs also mean the procurement of fewer new types of equipment. For example, between 1951 and 1960, the UK introduced twenty new types of combat aircraft; but for 1971–80, this number had declined to four new types (Kirkpatrick and Pugh, 1983). Such declines also create major policy problems, namely, the challenge of retaining a national equipment design capability (e.g. aerospace, nuclear submarines).

Inevitably, efforts have been made to 'control' cost growth with policy-makers introducing procurement initiatives which will 'solve' the problem. Bureaucrats in industry and government will soon adjust by adopting a 'fail-safe' approach to decisions by avoiding risk. Industry will resort to employing more auditors: Augustine proposed another law, namely, that 'Two-thirds of the Earth's surface is covered with water. The other third is covered with auditors from headquarters' (Augustine, 1987, p. 422).

1.14.2 Cost Levels

Unit cost growth does not capture absolute cost levels. Defence equipment is costly and some examples of cost levels and cost growth are shown in Table 1.3. Costly equipment includes aircraft carriers, nuclear-powered submarines, strategic bombers, combat aircraft, military transport aircraft and ballistic missiles. Cost increases are particularly high for aircraft, helicopters and missiles. However, cost data do not show the military capabilities of equipment (e.g. its operational performance in combat) although it is reasonable to assume that generally operational performance improves with cost but eventually, increments of performance are increasingly costly. Costs are also important because they form the defence economics problem. Cost levels and trends mean that policymakers cannot avoid choices. Defence budgets represent constraints on spending so that the purchase of a costly aircraft carrier or nuclear-powered submarine represents the sacrifice of alternative spending on, say, combat aircraft, helicopters and tanks. These are military choices faced by the armed forces but society also faces choices. The purchase of nuclear weapons involves the sacrifice of hospitals, schools and roads and government has to make such 'trade-offs': nuclear forces mean fewer schools and hospitals.

1.14.3 Production Costs, Scale and Learning Economies

Production costs vary with output. They comprise labour, capital (e.g. machinery), parts, components and materials. For example, firms involved in the production of combat aircraft require skilled labour for assembly operations plus engines, radar, landing gear and ejector seats. Unit production costs fall with greater output reflecting both scale and learning economies. Scale economies lead to falling unit costs as the scale of output is increased. Learning economies lead to lower unit production costs as the number of units produced is increased. Typical learning curves show reductions in unit costs of 10–15% for every doubling in total or cumulative output (Hartley and Sandler, 2001).[7]

Learning curves were originally estimated for the aircraft industry and widely used throughout the world's aerospace industries. They also apply to a range of defence equipment (e.g. electronics; tanks; warships) and to civil goods (e.g. machine tools; steel industry). Originally, an 80% learning curve was used widely in the aircraft industry showing that direct labour inputs declined by 20% for every doubling in the *cumulative* output of a given type of aircraft (e.g. cumulative output increasing from 2 to 4 to 8 to 16 to 32 units, etc.). Learning results from labour 'learning by doing' so improving productivity through repetition. It is characteristic of labour-intensive production methods and it becomes less important as firms adopt capital-intensive production methods and more outsourcing (Asher, 1956; Sandler and Hartley, 1995; Kirkpatrick, 2019).

1.14.4 Development Costs

Development costs comprise the costs of design, development and testing of prototypes followed by their modification and further testing until the required performance is achieved. To economists, development costs form fixed costs that are incurred regardless of the number of units produced and purchased. There is, though, a further perspective on development costs, involving a trade-off between time and cost. For a given level of technology (e.g. a given aircraft speed), time and costs are inputs with a 'trade-off' between total costs and time taken for development. Faster development is costlier while more leisurely

---

[7] The formula for learning is: $y = aX^{-b}$ where y= number of man hours for each unit produced; X= cumulative output (total number of units produced: not annual production); a= man hours for the first unit; b slope of the learning curve usually defined in relation to a doubling of cumulative output. US evidence suggests learning curves of 89%, which means reductions of 11% in unit costs for every doubling in cumulative output (Arena et al., 2008).

development is cheaper (i.e. a negative relationship between development cost and time to complete development for a given level of technology). Different levels of technology involve different trade-off curves. For example, a requirement for a faster aircraft involves a new trade-off curve requiring greater inputs of both time and costs. More technology is also more uncertain meaning that trade-off curves are not so well-defined and might become bands or blobs rather than single curves[8]. This approach provides an analytical framework that explains cost escalation in terms of urgency, modifications, unforeseen technical problems and contractor optimism (Tisdell and Hartley, 2008, p. 382).

Once development has been completed, the equipment proceeds to production, which forms a recurring or variable cost, varying with the number of units purchased. For each class of equipment (e.g. combat aircraft; armoured fighting vehicles), development costs tend to vary in proportion to unit production cost, but the ratio of development cost to unit production cost varies between classes of equipment. For combat aircraft, the ratio of development cost to unit production cost is in the region of 100 (varying between 80 and 140); for helicopters the ratio is 120; for military transport aircraft it is 40; for anti-tank weapons it is 25,000; for armoured fighting vehicles it is 250; and for warships it ranges between 0.8 and 2.5 (Kirkpatrick, 2019; Pugh, 2007). These ratios can be used to estimate the total costs of acquisition, namely, development and production costs using the following equation:

$$TC = (R+Q) \times UPC$$

where TC is total acquisition cost comprising total development and total production costs; R is the ratio of development cost to unit production cost; Q is quantity of output (production); and UPC is unit production cost. Using this equation, the total acquisition cost for the UK of a combat aircraft such as Typhoon might be £30 billion (Q = 200 units; UPC = £100 million per unit). Examples of equipment costs are shown in Table 1.3.

Development and production costs are part of the total or whole life-cycle costs of acquiring and operating defence equipment. Once the equipment has been delivered there are additional in-service costs comprising operations (e.g. training; exercises), repair and maintenance, modifications and mid-life updates. Some of these activities are undertaken 'in-house' and others are

---

[8] Economists use iso-quants analysis to represent the trade-off between time and cost. Each iso-quant is downward – sloping and represents a given level of technology or equipment performance. For a given iso-quant, faster development (e.g. an urgent requirement or 'crash' programme) involves higher cost that is immediately seen as one source of cost escalation. Or, if a more advanced project is required, there is a shift to a higher iso-quant requiring greater inputs of both time and cost, which is a further source of cost escalation.

Table 1.3 Defence equipment costs: levels and growth

Equipment type	Absolute cost (£s 2019 prices)	Annual rate of cost increase (%)
Sea systems		
Aircraft carrier	8.0B	3
Air defence ship	934 mn	2
Anti-submarine warfare ship	380 mn	2
SSBN (launch of nuclear missiles)	2.8B	NS
SSN (hunter-killer)	1.9B	1
Land		
Main battle tank	5.8mn	1
Armoured personnel carrier	876 K	2
Air		
Fighter/strike aircraft	102mn	4
Bomber aircraft (strategic)	3.7B	10
Primary trainer aircraft	8.8mn	7
Advanced trainer aircraft	24.8mn	4
Military transport/tanker aircraft	292mn	4
Reconnaissance UAV	36.5 K	6
Attack helicopter	35mn	5
Anti-submarine helicopter	29mn	6
Transport helicopter	23.4mn	4
Small arms		
Rifle	2.2 K	2
Machine gun	5.1 K	NS
Missiles		
Cruise missile	6.6mn	8
Ballistic missile	58mn	5

Notes:

i) NS is not statistically significant.

ii) Absolute costs in constant 2019 prices in pounds sterling: K is thousands; mn is millions; and B is billions. Constant prices are based on the UK Retail Price Index.

iii) Unit cost figures include development costs for warships (i.e. total acquisition costs comprising development and production). For all other equipment, unit costs are for unit production costs (i.e. excluding development cost).

iv) Cost increases are in specific costs: £s per ton for ships; £s per tonne for tanks and personnel carriers; and £s per kilogram for aircraft and missiles. These are units to measure the size of weapons as used by Pugh (2007). Cost figures are median values.

v) Cost data are based on projects worldwide for which there is published data but most projects are from the USA and Europe.

Source: Pugh (2007).

performed by outside contractors. Finally, there is disposal of equipment which varies between export sales and scrapping where scrapping ranges from sale for simple dismantling of conventional equipment to the more complex and costly task of disposing of nuclear weapons and other nuclear-powered systems (e.g. submarines). Overall, whole life cycle costs might be twice acquisition costs comprising development and production costs (e.g. depending on equipment types, its complexity and rate of use). For the UKs Typhoon combat aircraft acquisition costs of development and production were estimated to be £22.95 billion with total life-cycle costs estimated to be £39.6 billion (i.e. equipment acquisition costs were under 60% of total life-cycle costs (HCP 755, 2011)).

Operating costs for defence equipment also tend to rise. Operating cost growth for military aircraft and helicopters ranges between 3% and 7% per annum in real terms. This effect might be due to operating older equipment. For example, an aircraft (e.g. Hercules transport) with 7% annual real growth in costs per flying hour would be almost four times more expensive to operate at age 30 than at age 10 (Trunkey, 2019).

1.14.5 Defence Inflation

Defence inflation differs from intergenerational cost escalation. Defence inflation affects the money value of defence budgets and their buying power. It also affects money cost growth for specific equipment programmes (i.e. within a programme such as the F-35). Defence inflation shows the average rate of increase in pay and in the prices of all goods and services in the defence budget, after adjusting for changes in quality and quantity (MoD, 2017). It shows inflation in defence inputs. Estimates of UK defence inflation for 2004/5 to 2015/16 are presented in Table 1.4.

Defence inflation varies over time and between various inputs. In 2015/16, UK defence inflation was 3.9%. Most of this inflation was due to higher inflation in military and civilian labour costs which increased to 9.5% in 2015/16, mainly due to higher pension contributions for labour inputs. Within labour costs, the largest increase was for military personnel with an inflation rate of 11.5%. Comparisons with the GDP deflator and the Retail Prices Index (RPI) showed inflation rates of 0.8% and 1.1%, respectively for 2015/16, so that defence inflation was higher than UK general inflation. Defence inflation also differs between industries. In 2015/16, the UK inflation rate for all equipment was 1.3% with inflation rates of 2.0% for aerospace and spacecraft and 2.3% for mechanical engineering (MoD, 2014; Hartley and Solomon, 2016).

Table 1.4 UK defence inflation, 2005 to 2016

Financial year	Contracts (%)	Labour costs (%)	Defence inflation (%)
2005/6	3.4	5.6	4.1
2006/7	3.4	3.5	3.4
2007/8	3.7	4.3	3.9
2008/9	4.2	3.6	4.2
2009/10	2.5	4.0	3.2
2010/11	3.8	4.7	4.2
2011/12	3.4	3.4	3.4
2012/13	2.2	0.4	1.5
2013/14	2.4	1.5	2.1
2014/15	1.1	0.3	0.8
2015/16	1.3	9.5	3.9

Notes:
i) Cash Offices data are not shown.
ii) Each category is weighted: contracts at 670; labour costs at 315; and Cash Offices at 15 giving total weight of 1000.
iii) Financial year 2004/5 is the base year.
Source: MoD (2017).

Defence inflation has important policy and budget impacts. Efforts to control defence spending have sometimes led to annual budget changes based on the GDP deflator or RPI. While such policies will control the money value of defence budgets, they will affect its real value or buying power. For example, an increase in defence spending based on a GDP deflator of 2% when defence inflation is, say, 5% means a real terms reduction in defence spending. Defence inflation also affects other nations. For example, US defence inflation in 2015/16 was 1% (DoD, 2019).[9]

1.15 The Role of Technology: R&D Inputs

Technology is an input into the military production function with defence R&D funding the development costs of equipment. Typically, defence R&D is government-funded, especially for costly high technology equipment. Development work on a completely new and unknown project is risky. High costs, high risks with government as the sole buyer means that private firms and their shareholders are usually unwilling to provide private funds for developing

---

[9] It is difficult to obtain published data on defence inflation in other countries, with problems arising from translation.

such equipment. This unwillingness to provide private funds is reinforced where the government as sole buyer might cancel the project and where the equipment has no alternative users or buyers. It is also likely that funding the project will require all the private firm's assets. These features of defence R&D are reflected in the type of contracts used to fund development work on costly, high technology defence equipment (e.g. combat aircraft, missiles, warships and tanks). Traditionally, defence development work was funded using *cost-plus contracts* where the firm recovered all its costs regardless of their level plus an agreed profit rate. These contracts were notorious for inefficiency, cost overruns and delays (i.e. they were known as 'blank cheque' contracts). To respond to their inefficiency, various incentive elements were introduced into cost-plus contracts. For example, profits were offered as a fixed fee and not as a percentage of actual costs; or, performance targets were introduced, such as the fee being withheld until, say, an aircraft's first flight or a tank fired its first shell.

Some countries introduced more radical contract options for development work, including *target cost incentive contracts and fixed price contracts.* Target cost contracts with sharing ratios provide incentives to meet the originally agreed cost estimate. These contracts include a sharing ratio which ensures that cost savings or losses are shared in an agreed ratio between the government and contractor (e.g. a ratio of 80:20 where the government bears 80% of any cost overruns and receives 80% of any cost savings). Such contracts might also include a maximum price which indicates the government's maximum price liability beyond which further cost increases are borne solely by the contractor (Hartley, 2011, ch. 7; Hartley and Sandler, 2001, vol. II).

In contrast, fixed price contracts are high-powered incentive schemes compared with cost-plus contracts which are low-powered incentive schemes. Fixed price contracts for development shift risks to the contractor, which receives an initially agreed fixed sum of money on completion of the work (based on estimated costs plus a profit margin). If the contractor completed the work at less than the initially agreed sum, it retained the difference; but if its costs exceeded the original estimate, the contractor bears all the additional costs. A riskier variant of such contracts arises where a fixed price is agreed for the total package procurement comprising design, development, production and support (or it might be for development and production) with the contract embracing price, performance and delivery commitments. US examples were the C-5 Galaxy military transport aircraft and the Spruance-class destroyers. Fixed prices for total package procurement were a reaction to the previous cost-plus regime: their aim was to end the practice where firms deliberately bid low prices to win a competition and they aimed to end 'optimism bias'. The results were different: successful bidding contractors encountered major design and technical problems, leading to cost overruns and delays and major financial problems (e.g. possible bankruptcy of major firms). In contrast, the UK used total package procurement successfully for the acquisition of its Hawk jet trainer aircraft.

Defence R&D is subject to its own R&D production function. This shows that today's defence R&D determines future military equipment quality or performance with its impact on future defence output. The R&D–equipment relationship is a positive relationship subject to diminishing returns and substantial lags (curvi-linear). It suggests that current military equipment quality was determined by defence R&D spending some ten to fifteen years ago. Equipment quality can be converted into a time advantage. For instance, over the period 1991–2001, US military equipment was six years ahead of the UK, seven years ahead of France and twelve years ahead of Sweden (Middleton et al., 2006).[10]

Defence R&D can have revolutionary impacts on military forces, military capabilities and defence industries. Examples include aircraft, missiles, rockets and space systems. The aircraft industry emerged as a new industry in 1903 and it comprised a number of one-person firms who pioneered and invented manned flying machines. The early pioneers explored new ideas with varying degrees of success and failure (e.g. aircraft crashes). The First World War provided a major change in aviation leading to new ideas, faster aircraft and aircraft with longer ranges and greater weapons carrying capability. Air Forces emerged as new branches of the armed forces alongside armies and navies. Similarly, aircraft industries were created and became new entrants into defence industries. The Second World War gave another impetus to the aircraft industry with massive increases in demand for military aircraft, the emergence of jet engines and the first generation of cruise missiles and long-range rockets (V-1 and V-2 weapons). After the Second World War, there followed an expansion of civil aviation using technologies developed originally for the military (e.g. jet engines; radar), the emergence of cruise missiles and ICBMs with nuclear weapons and space exploration, including the Moon landings. The aircraft industry was re-named the aerospace industry and it was dominated by a small number of large firms (Hartley, 2014).

New technology can render obsolescent traditional methods of warfare. Nuclear-powered submarines replaced battleships; new communication systems replaced balloons, pigeons and human messengers; nuclear weapons

---

[10] The defence R&D production function can be expressed: $E = f(R\&D; Z)$ where E is military equipment quality; R&D is defence R&D; and Z is all other relevant factors (e.g. total non-R&D military spending; previous military projects representing previous experience).

replaced large conventional forces; and UAVs and drones have replaced manned aircraft for surveillance roles. Much depends on the willingness of the armed forces and defence industries to adjust to change and adopt new technology. Ultimately, a failure to adopt such technologies leads to defeat in conflict.

1.15.1 Spin-offs

Defence R&D might contribute to wider economic benefits in the form of technical spin-offs and spill-overs (also known as external economies or external benefits). There are numerous examples including jet engines, the internet, avionics, radar, computers, electronics, civil airliners and composite materials (e.g. being applied to racing car, fishing rod, tennis racquet production). These beneficial externalities form part of the wider economic benefits of defence spending. However, there are at least two problems with using spin-offs to justify defence spending. First, technical spin-offs are not the main aim of defence spending, which is about peace, protection and security. Second, a list of examples of spin-offs' fails to address the major question of the market value of such spin-offs and whether there are better alternative uses of defence R&D resources (scientists and laboratories). For example, instead of working on research into nuclear weapons, scientists might be employed on research into discovering new medicines. Identifying alternatives is easy, but difficulties arise in creating incentives for resources to move to other activities (e.g. a defence scientist might not want to work on researching new medicines).

1.16 Capital Inputs

In the military production function, capital inputs consist of defence equipment, especially lethal equipment (e.g. artillery; combat aircraft; missiles; warships), together with other goods and services. Also included are communications systems, such as space communications, as well as land for military bases (army camps, airfields and ports) and training areas. Lethal equipment is distinctive in that it is usually bought by governments. Exceptions include private armies (mercenaries), terrorists and their organisations, and criminal gangs and organised crime groups (e.g. Mafia). Often, lethal equipment is bought to a government's special requirements and does not exist in the market place: it has to be designed, developed and produced specially to meet a government's operational requirements (e.g. for a specific type of tank or submarine). Other goods and services include a whole range of civil goods and services that are bought by armed forces. Examples include computers, housing, office furniture, motor cars, construction equipment and services such as accountancy, management consultancy and transport. Such goods and services usually already exist and are bought and sold in competitive civil markets (e.g. motor cars; computers). Similarly, land can be purchased in open markets, although governments can impose restrictions on its use (e.g. firing ranges). Annual purchases of capital inputs are usually shown in a nation's annual defence budget (Hartley and Sandler, 2001, vol II).

1.16.1 Defence Budgets

Defence budgets show a nation's annual defence spending. In democracies, they provide one means of informing citizens and voters about how much is spent on defence and on its armed forces. Not all nations publish information on their annual defence spending (e.g. some African states and North Korea). Transparency International publishes examples of nations with low and high transparency in their defence budgets. Examples of low transparency nations in their defence budgets include Algeria, Angola, Cambodia, China, Egypt, Iraq, Nigeria, Pakistan, Saudi Arabia and Serbia. Countries with high transparency include Bosnia and Herzegovina, France, Germany, New Zealand, Norway, South Africa, Sweden, UK and USA (TI, 2011).

How well do defence budgets allow policymakers and voters to assess efficiency in a nation's defence spending? Much depends on the form in which the national defence budget is published. Here, there are a number of types ranging from input budgets to output budgets to resource accounting budgets. Further problems arise since definitions of defence spending can vary between nations: not all nations use the same definition of defence spending and definitions differ between data sources (UN, IMF, NATO, SIPRI, IISS) (Hartley, 2018a).

Input budgets provide only limited information for assessing efficiency in defence spending. They show expenditure on pay for service personnel, reserves and civilians, spending on production and research together with spending on movements, supplies, works, buildings and land and spending on miscellaneous services. Some of these spending categories are helpful: for instance, labour and capital costs are identified but other inputs are much less useful unless decision makers are concerned about the armed forces consumption of food and fuel (see Table 1.5).

Published input budgets fail to address at least two problems when assessing efficiency in the use of defence resources. First, no outputs are shown other than the vague, general heading of 'defence'. At best, data might be available on the numbers of military personnel in each of the armed forces and their equipment by types and numbers, for example: numbers of soldiers, tanks and fighting

Table 1.5 Input and output defence budgets

INPUT BUDGET		OUTPUT BUDGET	
Item	**Costs (£mn 2018 prices)**	**Item**	**Costs (£mn 2018 prices)**
Pay of service personnel	7,503	Nuclear strategic forces	2,962
Pay of reserves	431	Navy general purpose combat forces	5,646
Pay of civilians	5,037	European theatre ground forces	7,413
Movements	1,045	Other army combat forces	508
Supplies	2,389	Air force general purpose forces	8,126
Production & Research	17,201	Research and Development	5,004
a) Production	*13,529*		
b) Research	*3,672*		
Works, buildings, land	3,419	Training	3,159
Miscellaneous services	392	Equipment support and facilities in UK	2,520
Non-effective charges	1,387	War and contingency stocks	1,060
		Other support functions	9,274
Total	**38,814**	**Total**	**46,884**

Notes:

i) Input budget is based on UK for 1965–6 with costs converted to 2018 prices based on UK RPI.

ii) For UK, input budget shows total spending on production and research and its components separately.

iii) Output budget is for UK in 1991–2 with costs converted to 2018 prices using UK RPI.

iv) For the UK, the output budget was known as a Functional Costing budget. This budget excludes Miscellaneous expenditure and receipts (£215 million in 2018 prices).

v) The UK Functional Costing budget shows only major programmes. Its published version also shows various sub-programmes each with detailed costings (e.g. naval general purpose combat forces comprises aircraft carriers, destroyers, frigates and submarines each with their costings).

Source: Hartley (2018).

vehicles in the army; numbers of sailors, warships and submarines for the navy; and numbers of air force personnel and various types of aircraft squadrons (combat aircraft; maritime patrol; helicopters; transport aircraft). Second, the input budget information does not show the relation between inputs and outputs nor the opportunities for factor substitution. No information is presented on the costs of nuclear versus conventional forces; nor on the costs and implications of substituting reserve forces for regulars. At best, input budgets focus on substitution possibilities between such items as pay, petrol, movements, food and buildings with no information on the output effects of such substitutions.

1.16.2 Programme Budgets

The economist's model of defence budgets focuses on the costs of specific inputs and outputs and is known as output budgeting or programme budgeting (Hitch and McKean, 1960). Programme budgeting or a Planning, Programming and Budgeting System (PPBS) provides decision makers with an information framework for assessing defence choices as reflected in objectives, defence outputs and their costs. It is in complete contrast to traditional input budgets. PPBS was first introduced into the US Department of Defense in 1961 (under Robert McNamara and Charles Hitch: see Table 1.5). It combines planning, programming and budgeting decisions in defence choices, but it does not make choices: decision makers still need to make choices.

Programme or output budgeting seeks answers to four questions that are key to assessing efficiency in resource-use in defence. First, what are the objectives of defence and can these objectives be presented in a set of programmes? Second, what are the costs of each of these programmes? Costs are current annual and expected life-cycle costs. Third, what are the outputs or results of each programme? Fourth, what are the alternative methods of achieving each programme and what are the costs and outputs of each alternative? Cost-effectiveness studies are used to assess the alternatives. In assessing defence budgets, it is necessary to distinguish between publicly available information and what is available within defence ministries. While public data are limited by security considerations, considerably more information is available within the armed forces and defence ministries which forms the basis for defence choices.

Programme budgets show more economically relevant information than traditional input budgets. They show the costs of various military forces and capabilities; they can be used to identify the impact of cuts in defence spending; and they show opportunities for substitution between military forces (see Table 1.5). However, limitations remain. Some programme budgets are a mixture of outputs and inputs. For example, the programmes shown in Table 1.5 comprise six programmes which are based on combat forces with the rest being pro-grammes which are support activities not allocated to front-line units. Alternative programmes can be arranged such as nuclear forces, naval combat forces, land combat forces, air combat forces together with special forces. Each major programme would include inputs of reserve forces, training, R&D spending, production facilities, stocks and other support functions: inputs which form separate programmes in Table 1.5.

Further limitations of programme budgeting arise from the absence of any measurable defence output in the form of a money valuation of peace, protection and security and the probability of survival in conflicts. Nor are the spending figures in output budgets (or other forms of budgeting) based on cost-minimising behaviour. They are likely to be X-inefficient since individuals and groups in the armed forces lack incentives to minimise costs.

1.16.3 Resource Budgets

In some nations (e.g. UK), the continuous search for efficiency improvements in the defence economy led to the introduction of resource accounting and budgeting (RAB). RAB involved a shift from cash budgets to resource budgets which involved two major changes. First, resource accounting meant that costs are accounted for when resources are consumed rather than when cash payments are made. Second, resource costs include interest on capital and depreciation of fixed assets. The result of resource accounting is that individual budget holders will bear costs that were previously hidden from them and borne centrally. Examples include the costs of land, buildings and equipment stocks (e.g. 'too many' army training areas; surplus buildings; and 'excessive' stock holdings).

RAB aims to ensure that the 'full costs' of inputs will be identified and matched with outputs in the form of front-line units so increasing pressures to improve efficiency in the armed forces. There will be pressure to dispose of surplus defence assets (e.g. close and sell surplus military bases, making them available for new house building). Under cash budgets, where not all resource costs were identified, there were incentive to 'hoard' surplus land, buildings and real estate. RAB also provides a balance sheet showing the book value of defence fixed assets, mostly comprising fighting equipment (aircraft, tanks and warships) and the defence estate. Predictably, RAB provides valuable information for accountants but it cannot be assumed that adopting private sector accounting methods will automatically change behaviour leading to improved efficiency in the armed forces. Efficiency in the private sector requires competition, profit and loss incentives and penalties and a reasonably efficient capital market. The armed forces are faced with a further limitation when assessing their efficiency, namely, the absence of market prices to measure the value of defence output. Ultimately, the major barrier to raising efficiency in the armed forces arises from individuals and groups who will adjust to any changes and 'play any games'.

1.17 Equipment Procurement

Capital inputs in the form of equipment are procured through procurement policy. Nations buying new defence equipment have to make choices between the extremes of buying from their national firms or importing from foreign firms. Much depends on their demand requirements and the technology level of their national defence industry. Requirements for relatively simple and low technology weapons might be supplied by their national defence firms (e.g. patrol boats or rifles). More complex, high technology weapons might not be available from domestic suppliers requiring governments to buy from abroad (e.g. combat aircraft, helicopters, missiles, tanks and warships). Or, some nations use their national demand requirements to create a domestic defence industrial base capable of developing and producing high technology weapons (e.g. Indian, Japanese and South Korean aerospace industries). Creating such a national defence industry can be costly and takes time. Without such an industrial base, governments have to import foreign equipment off-the-shelf.

1.17.1 Imports and Offsets

Importing foreign defence equipment is not as simple as appears. The foreign buyer requires information and knowledge about its equipment requirements (e.g. type of combat aircraft, its speed, range, altitude, armaments and weapons carrying capacity) where the selling firm will be the expert in such knowledge (reflecting information asymmetries). The foreign buyer might also have additional requirements for work-sharing on the project. Work-sharing might take the form of some type of *offset* where the buying nation requires some work either directly on the equipment being bought or indirectly on some other defence or civil projects. Offsets enable a buying nation to obtain some work share by re-distributing work from the selling nation to the buying nation with questions arising about the efficiency implications of such a re-allocation. In some cases, re-allocation can be inefficient as work is re-allocated to higher-cost suppliers in the buying nation. Or, re-allocation can be efficient where work is awarded to lower-cost suppliers (Hartley and Sandler, 2001, vols II and III; Sandler and Hartley, 1995, ch. 9).

Nations importing foreign equipment might obtain a work share through *licensed production* of the equipment. Licensed production represents a direct offset where the buying nation builds foreign-designed equipment under licence in its own country. For licensed production, the aim might be to build all the equipment locally or to build some parts and/or undertake final assembly within the importing nation. Licences usually require a fee to be paid for the licence (e.g. as a contribution to government or privately provided R&D costs). A variant of licensed production is *co-production* where a group of participating nations each purchases the same equipment and produces parts of each nation's order. An example of co-production was the four nation European consortium which acquired the US F-16 aircraft. European industry was awarded work on 10% of the USAF order for 650 F-16s, 40% of the work on the 348 F-16s bought by the Europeans and 15% of export sales. This sharing arrangement guaranteed European industry 58% of the value of the European order (Belgium, Denmark, Netherlands and Norway).

Licensed and co-production usually involve cost penalties compared with buying directly 'off-the-shelf' from the original equipment manufacturer. Cost penalties for licensed production reflect entry costs, the costs of transferring technology, short production runs and the loss of both scale and learning economies. The US-European co-production of the F-16 was estimated to cost the Europeans a 34% cost penalty compared with a direct purchase from General Dynamics (Rich et al., 1981). There are offsetting economic and military benefits from licensed and co-production. Economic benefits include jobs, technology transfer (e.g. management and production technologies) and import-savings. There are also savings in R&D resources, which would other-wise have been required for an independent national programme. Military benefits include independence and support for a nation's defence industrial base and the benefits of equipment standardisation.

1.17.2 International Collaboration

International collaboration represents a further procurement option. It involves two or more nations sharing development costs and combining production orders. Collaboration is a response to rising unit costs of equipment and small production orders. France, Germany, Italy and the UK have extensive experience of international arms collaboration, mostly for aerospace projects. Examples include the Anglo-French Jaguar strike aircraft, the French-German Alpha Jet, the UK-German-Italian-Spanish Typhoon combat aircraft, the seven nation A400 M airlifter and various collaborative missile projects.

Theoretically, collaboration offers cost savings reflected in both development and production costs. Consider the case of two nations agreeing to the equal sharing of all development and production costs for a combat aircraft. Development costs might be £20 billion with each nation requiring 200 units. Collaboration means that each nation will contribute £10 billion for development so saving £10 billion each compared with an identical national project. There are further savings in production, where a doubling of output leads to economies of scale and learning which might reduce unit production costs by some 10%, where unit costs might be, say, £100 million per unit. This is an 'ideal case' or perfect collaboration where it is assumed that everything else remains unchanged between a national project and collaboration.

In reality, perfect collaboration is never achieved. Actual international collaboration is characterised by inefficiencies. Political markets and producer interest groups interfere with a desire for an economically efficient collaboration. Work-sharing rules lead to work being allocated on political criteria rather than on the basis of competitiveness and comparative advantage. Each partner nation will demand its fair share of each component of high technology work on the project. For a combat aircraft, each will demand a share of development work on the airframe, engine and avionics. Partners will require duplicate flight testing centres and duplicate final assembly lines. An elaborate committee structure will be created to manage the project, with decision making based on unanimity or majority voting rules, further contributing to delays and cost increases. Two rules of thumb have been formulated for estimating collaboration inefficiencies. First, for cost inefficiencies, the square root rule suggests that the extra development costs of collaboration can be estimated by taking the square root of the number of nations in the project. A four-nation project might raise total development costs to twice their level for a similar national project; even so, there would still be savings to each partner nation compared with a national venture. Second, on delays there is the cube root rule where the total development time and delays on collaboration can be estimated by the cube root of the number of nations on the project. This rule suggests that a seven-nation project might take almost twice the time for development compared with a national venture (e.g. A400 M) (Hartley, 2011, 2019).

Evaluating collaboration is problematic. Their benefits and costs need to be identified to determine whether they have been worthwhile. While data are usually available on costs, estimating benefits is considerably more difficult. Each partner nation will pursue different policy objectives comprising a variety of benefits and will place different (subjective) valuations on benefits. Methodological problems arise from the counterfactual issue of what would have happened in the absence of a collaborative project? Would each partner nation have developed and produced an identical or similar national programme or would it have imported directly from the USA with or without a work-sharing agreement? Comparisons between collaborative and similar national projects require that comparators be available. This is possible for combat aircraft where comparisons are available between the collaborative Typhoon and similar national projects such as the French Rafale, the Swedish Gripen and various US aircraft (F-15, F-16, F-18, F-22 and F-35) (Hartley, 2014).

Rising equipment costs provide continued economic inducements for collaboration. However, there remains considerable scope for improving the efficiency of collaborative ventures. Possibilities for efficiency improvements include the award of contracts to a single prime contractor, using competition to select the prime contractor; work-shares based on efficiency and competitive criteria; restricting the number of equal partners to two nations; and a willingness to extend collaboration to nations outside Europe. But competition has its limitations as an efficient procurement policy.

1.17.3 Role and Limitations of Competition

Equipment procurement policy involves various choices relating to the choice of equipment type (performance specifications), choice of contractor, choice of procurement method (competitive versus non-competitive) and choice of when to buy. These are choices of what to buy, who from, how and when to buy. Government decides whether to use competition to determine these choices and whether competition should be restricted to domestic firms or whether foreign firms should be allowed to bid. In principle, competition determines both prices and profitability for the project.

Often, competition is not available due to a unique product specification or the national industry is monopolistic and government chooses not to allow foreign firms to bid for the contract. In these circumstances, contracts are non-competitive raising a range of problems to be solved. Non-competitive contracts are negotiated contracts between a procurement agency (buyer) and a selected supplier (often a national defence firm). The negotiators have to determine the price and profits for the contract where negotiations will involve 'game playing' as each party seeks maximum advantage using strategies of threats, bluff, chicken, first mover advantage and 'tit-for-tat'. For example, the firm might threaten to withdraw from the bid while government might threaten to cancel the project. The outcome of successful negotiations will be an agreement in the form of a contract specifying what is being bought, when it is to be delivered, at what price and agreed profits with penalties for breach of contract. Typically, prices for non-competitive contracts are based on costs for both development and production work plus an agreed profit rate. But there are problems in determining costs and profits. On costs, choices are needed as to whether to use estimated or actual costs for both development and production work. Development work can be highly uncertain and if prices are based on estimated costs, then the contractor bears all the risks of cost overruns (e.g. fixed price contracts). Whereas, if prices are based on actual costs, the government bears all the risks of cost overruns (e.g. cost-plus contracts). This is not all: profits have to be determined for non-competitive contracts. Here, options include profits based on some percentage of either estimated or actual costs; but the percentage rate has to be determined. The percentage rate might be based on the average rate of return for all firms in the economy or based on the cost of capital (Hartley, 2018b).

Even where competition is possible, it has at least four limitations. First, one of the losing firms in a competition can always acquire the winning firm (via a take-over). Second, a contractor might bid a low or loss-making price with the intention of recouping losses on the price of spares (the equipment is cheap but you pay for the spares). Third, the domestic defence industry might be mono-polistic so that introducing competition requires foreign firms being allowed to bid for national contracts. Foreign firms require some reasonable prospect of success in any competition (i.e. that they are not being used as 'stalking horses') to induce them to submit attractive bids (bids are not costless). But, awarding contracts to foreign firms imposes costs on the national defence industry. Fourth, once a competition has been completed, the winning firm becomes a monopoly supplier. There are options to safeguard against such monopoly. For example, on completion of development work, the production contract can be subject to further competition or competition might continue into the devel-opment phase if the development contract is divided between two rival suppliers (duplicate development). These options are not costless. If bidders are not guaranteed production work, they might raise their prices at the initial bidding stage. Similarly, duplicate development is costly, requiring the funding of two or more development projects. During the 1950s, the UK used a duplicate devel-opment policy for fighter and bomber aircraft. This policy partly reflected the need for an insurance against project failure. As a result, the UK developed two fighter aircraft (Hunter and Swift) and three V-bombers (Valiant, Vulcan and Victor). In the fighter example, the Swift failed to meet its performance targets and was cancelled but the Hunter was available as a replacement.

A variant of duplicate development was introduced by the USA in the form of its 'fly before you buy' policy for aircraft selection. This involved competition between rival designs before the selection of two firms to bid for a prototype contract leading to a final choice based on a fly-off between the rival aircraft. The fly-off retained competition up to the final selection point after which the successful bidder became a monopoly supplier. The current Lockheed Martin F-35 Lightning II resulted from a fly-off competition between Boeing and Lockheed Martin.

Competition is subject to further limitations arising from the influence of producer groups and from legal requirements. The bidding phase of competition will be subject to contractors lobbying government to influence the contract award. Where foreign firms are involved in a competition, major domestic defence contractors will stress the benefits of a national procurement in the form of domestic jobs, technology, balance of payments contributions and security of supply. Such claims need to be subject to critical scrutiny. Economists will point to the costs of achieving such benefits and the range of alternative means available for creating jobs, technology, exports and providing security of supply. For example, other national industries, such as motor cars, computers, electronics and pharmaceuticals, provide such benefits as jobs, technology and exports. Benefits such as security of supply might be achieved by membership of a military alliance, through international diplomacy and by stock-piling quantities of foreign weapons. A comprehensive economic evaluation of procurement requires that decisions be subject to a cost–benefit analysis focusing on costs, including externalities and on the valuation of benefits.

Further limitations of competition arise from a country's legal constraints. Competition awards might be subject to legal review allowing decisions to be questioned and reversed. An example occurred with the USAF competition for a new air tanker fleet. In early 2008, after a competition between Boeing and Northrop Grumman/EADS, the USAF selected the Northrop Grumman/EADS bid. Boeing objected to the decision and following a series of admissions by the USAF of flaws in the bidding process and a major Boeing public relations campaign, the tanker contract was re-opened. For the renewed competition, Airbus/EADS bid without Northrop Grumman and competed against Boeing. In early 2011, the USAF announced that the Boeing bid was selected. Following selection, the Boeing bid was subject to delays, cost overruns and cost penalties imposed on Boeing for contract failures.

1.17.4 Arms Exports

Arms exports form one part of the international trade in arms: arms imports are the other part. Critics condemn arms exports and imports for contributing to regional arms races and local conflict; they are viewed as supporting oppressive

Table 1.6 Major arms exporters and importers, 2018

Country	Arms exports (US$mn)	Country	Arms imports (US$mn)
USA	10,508	Saudi Arabia	3,810
Russia	6,409	Australia	1,572
France	1,768	China	1,566
Germany	1,277	India	1,539
Spain	1,188	Egypt	1,484
S Korea	1,083	Algeria	1,318
China	1,040	S Korea	1,317
UK	741	UAE	1,101
Israel	707	Qatar	816
Italy	711	Pakistan	777
TOTAL	**27,587**	**TOTAL**	**27,587**

Notes:
i) Top 10 exporters and importers are shown. Totals are for world.
ii) Figures are trend indicator values, which show only the volume and not the value of arms transfers.
Source: SIPRI (2019)

regimes with poor human rights records; and for poor nations, they divert resources from economic development.

Data on arms exports and imports in 2018 are shown in Table 1.6. The USA, Russia and France form the world's top three arms exporters with Saudi Arabia, Australia and China forming the corresponding arms importing nations. These are cross-section data and the rankings change over time. Further problems arise with arms trade data. Sometimes data are for orders and not actual sales; the sales can be based on acquisition or include a range of support packages (e.g. training; supply of spares); and unit prices might be for unit production costs only or include a premium for R&D costs (Hartley and Sandler, 2001, vol. III).

Arms exports are often presented as a wider economic benefit from a national defence industry. Exports also provide jobs and maintain a national defence industry capability. Arms exports might also enable a national defence industry to achieve economies of scale and learning. Without exports, national governments would need to provide other means of retaining their industrial capability, each involving costs. Examples of such options include additional production orders for existing equipment; ordering technology demonstrators or prototypes; and the mothballing of plant and equipment.

1.18 The Economics of Military Outsourcing

Military outsourcing involves the transfer to private contractors of activities traditionally undertaken 'in-house' by the armed forces. The result is private firms replacing public sector organisations, representing a substitution of private organisations for public enterprises and activities. As a result, private firms provide inputs for military outputs: they assume responsibility for buying labour and capital inputs. Military outsourcing can be analysed as a public procurement problem and consideration is given to whether the public sector is inefficient. Outsourcing is a novel policy initiative that illustrates the opportunities for demonstrating the application of economic analysis and critical evaluation. The UK has considerable experience of outsourcing, which is reviewed in this section, but other nations such as Australia, Canada, Europe and the USA also have experience of the policy.

1.18.1 Definitions and Concepts

The defence economics problem requires difficult choices. One policy option is the search for increased efficiency within which military outsourcing offers opportunities for efficiency savings. Military outsourcing in the UK has been subject to various definitions, ranging from market testing to contractorisation, private finance initiatives (PFIs) and public-private partnerships (PPPs). It results in the substitution of private firms for 'in-house' public sector organisations. It also involves issues of public (state) versus private *finance* and public versus private *provision*. Here, the extremes range from government-funded and government-provided (owned) activities such as the army, navy and air force to activities that are wholly financed and provided by private firms (e.g. satellite communication services for the armed forces). Interestingly, defence is an example of a public good which traditionally has involved both public finance and public provision. Outsourcing demonstrates the opportunities for both private finance and private provision of some defence activities: they have resulted in the UK Ministry of Defence (MoD) and the armed forces shifting from 'make to buy'.

A taxonomy for military outsourcing is shown in Table 1.7. This focuses on the distinction between government (state) and private finance and provision for different types of defence activity. At one extreme, the state both finances and provides the whole range of assets, goods and services for both combat missions and support provided by the armed forces. This is the 'in-house' monopoly solution, which is typical of most nations. The other extreme involves the private sector both financing and providing the inputs for all combat and support activities. This is a controversial option but, in principle, there is no reason why

Table 1.7 In-house versus outsourcing: a taxonomy

	Buildings	Equipment	Other goods	Services	Support	Combat missions
State finance/ state provision	YES	YES	YES	YES	YES	YES
State finance/ private provision	YES	YES	YES	YES	YES	Possible
Private finance/ private provision	YES	YES	YES	YES	YES	Possible

combat missions could not be privately financed and privately provided. This is not to suggest the desirability of such an arrangement: it is simply recognised as a logical possibility and one which needs to be critically evaluated (hence, the options are given question marks). Also, the various defence activities in Table 1.7 can be further sub-divided to identify other factor inputs, especially whether labour inputs comprise military or civilian personnel. For example, buildings might involve the private contractor assuming responsibility for management, maintenance, repairs and security guarding. Similarly, some equipment might be maintained and repaired by either civilian or military personnel. Within private provision, a further distinction is required between competitive and non-competitive markets since market structure affects efficiency: private monopolies are inefficient.

The taxonomy in Table 1.7 raises two broad questions. First, why do governments out-source or contract-out some activities and undertake others 'in-house'? Second, what are the boundaries (limits) of government and private sector activities in defence? The answers to these questions involve a choice between private firms and public agencies where this choice involves:

- *private firms*, which offer high-powered efficiency incentives, but there are costs of contracting. These efficiency incentives are maximised under competitive (contestable) markets;
- *public agencies/organisations* which are characterised by low-powered efficiency incentives but which are good on loyalty and trust (e.g. sovereign-type transactions undertaken by government).

1.18.2 A public procurement problem

Military outsourcing can be viewed as a public procurement problem. As such it combines the skills and disciplines of economics and law. Economists formulate policy rules for efficient public procurement and government contracting which involves economic analysis of such issues as the following.

i) What to buy; from whom; and how to buy? This involves the choice of project, contractor and type of contract.

ii) The make or buy choice, namely, the choice between outsourcing and internal provision ('in-house').

iii) The role of competitive tendering as a mechanism for determining prices, promoting innovation and 'policing' profits.

iv) The efficiency implications of alternative types of contracts (e.g. fixed price versus cost-plus).

v) The need to regulate profits on non-competitive contracts and the appropriate regulatory rules (e.g. a maximum rate of return on capital or on costs).

vi) Recognition that public procurement can be used as a barrier to trade (i.e. government as a source of market failure).

vii) Public procurement provides opportunities for private sector corruption and bribery compared with possible inefficiencies and corruption associated with 'in-house' provision.

Lawyers then have to convert these often-vague economic principles into a set of rules and contractual arrangements which are legally enforceable. The result is a voluntarily negotiated and agreed contract between buyer and seller which requires the contractor to deliver a specific product or service within a specified time-period in return for an agreed payment.

1.18.3 The Policy Problem: An Inefficient Public Sector?

In-house public sector activities and organisations can be regarded as public monopolies. Since they are not subject to competition and rivalry, in-house public monopolies will be characterised by monopoly prices, inefficiency and a failure to innovate. Public choice analysis reinforces propositions about government inefficiency and the possibility of government failure. In this model, governments are vote-maximisers and bureaucracies are budget-maximisers, which are likely to exaggerate the demand for their preferred services and under-estimate their costs (e.g. defence ministries exaggerating the enemy's missile threat or the threat from international terrorism and under-estimating the costs of new weapons systems). Vote-sensitive government ministers will need to demonstrate that they are successful managers. For example, they can appear to demonstrate success by selecting performance indicators that can be easily achieved. However, performance indicators can give unexpected and sometimes perverse and undesirable outcomes (e.g. in the health sector, the claim that the operation was a success but the patient died!). Performance indicators also provide incentives to cheat and manipulate the statistics. As a means of assessing public sector efficiency, performance indicators need to be used carefully and critically.

Comparisons with the private sector provide a further reason why the public sector is likely to be inefficient. In the private sector, efficiency incentives are provided by the profit motive, by competition and rivalry and by the capital market with its threat of take-over and bankruptcy. These features are absent from the public sector. In defence, there is only one army, navy and air force each with a monopoly of land, sea and air forces (i.e. there is no rivalry). Military commanders are not entrepreneurs rewarded or penalised through profits and losses; nor can military units be subject to take-over or suffer bankruptcy (i.e. there are no capital market incentives/penalties). Yet, defence is a major user of scarce resources so that it is relevant to question the efficiency with which it uses society's scarce resources. While the public sector lacks entrepreneurship and profit incentives, its managers cannot avoid the need to make difficult choices under uncertainty. For defence policymakers, the uncertainties are great, involving the need to assemble a range of armed forces capable of meeting a variety of unknown and unknowable future threats over a long time horizon (e.g. typically, fifteen to twenty years but often longer).

Since debates about make or buy choices depend on efficiency implications, a definition of efficiency is required. Economists define efficiency to embrace two aspects.

i) *Technical efficiency* which focuses on the lowest-cost method of achieving a given output (in terms of quantity and/or quality). Typically, least-cost can be achieved by 'opening-up' markets to competition, with evidence suggesting cost savings of some 20% from competitive tendering. For example, private contractors might be able to provide catering, cleaning and transport services at lower-cost than 'in-house' provision by all-volunteer military personnel. In this way, civilian labour replaces military labour.

ii) *Allocative efficiency* which involves selecting the output that is socially desirable. The rule for an optimal output requires that marginal benefits equal marginal costs. But in the public sector, who determines what is socially desirable? In private competitive markets, firms respond to the tastes and preferences of large numbers of consumers. In contrast, in the public sector, it is elected politicians and civil servants (acting as agents) who interpret the wishes of the electorate (principals). And we know that the voting mechanism has its limitations as a means of expressing voter preferences for public sector goods and services and their quality. For defence policy, the allocative efficiency question requires judgements on the 'appropriate' level of defence spending and its associated 'output'.

While suggesting that the public sector can be inefficient, it cannot be assumed that the private sector is always efficient. Private markets can fail. Market failure can result from imperfections (e.g. monopoly, entry barriers) and externalities, including public goods. Also, the economists perfectly competitive model of efficiency has its limitations. The standard textbook model of perfect competition gives entrepreneurs little scope and opportunity for actual decision-making: there is no uncertainty, no surprise, no innovation and no entrepreneurship. The textbook economic model assumes that entrepreneurs have to produce a given product at a given price and to select the profit-maximising output, so providing little opportunity for entrepreneurship!

Debates about 'in-house' versus private sector provision also raise issues of methodology and the precise basis for comparisons. Typically, in such debates, private industry takes an 'ideal' model of a perfectly competitive private enterprise economy which is then compared with an actual model of an imperfect public sector (or state organisation). In contrast, critics present an 'ideal' model of a perfect public sector (or state organisation) compared with an imperfect private enterprise system. In reality, the relevant comparison is between two imperfect systems and forms of organisation and ownership where all modes of organisation are flawed.

1.18.4 PFI and PPP

The PFI involves private finance replacing state finance for capital projects. Instead of purchasing and owning capital assets, MoD agreed to the private sector financing the creation of the asset with MoD leasing it in return for annual rental payments (i.e. contracts for services). Under PFI, private industry commits to financing the often large up-front capital costs of a project and also commits to the provision of services to an agreed standard over many years. Only where PFI is shown to be inappropriate or uneconomic will the use of MoD capital resources be considered.

Initially, six areas were identified for PFI, namely, training, property and accommodation, information technology, equipment, support services, and utilities (Cmnd 3223, 1996, p. 89). Although dedicated war fighting equipment may be beyond the scope of PFI, little else is 'off-limits' including support for front-line units.

The next development in the UK was PPP, which extended the concept of partnership with private industry to embrace other approaches, especially the opportunities for raising revenue from the commercial exploitation of MoD assets and innovative forms of partnership between MoD and the private sector. PPP can embrace elements of PFI, contracting-out, commercial exploitation and involves activities as well as assets. For example, a PPP solution for rebuilding the Colchester Garrison showed that rebuilding could be completed within five years compared with some fifteen years under conventional procurement (and PPP offered other potential benefits). In some cases, PFI and PPPs are not appropriate, such as where some skills and capabilities are unique to defence and scale economies cannot be shared between MoD and the private sector. In such circumstances, MoD will purchase the assets needed, own them and manage them throughout their life-cycle (e.g. war fighting equipment).

1.18.5 Examples of PFI/PPP in UK Defence

Many of the UK's defence PFI/PPP projects have involved buildings (e.g. family accommodation and refurbishment of MoD main building) and training services; but there have been some more novel developments including strategic sealift and military satellite communications (Skynet 5). Examples of UK PFI projects embrace attack helicopter training, defence fixed telecommunications services, strategic sealift, heavy equipment transporters and combat aircraft simulators.

Some novel and innovatory PFI/PPP agreements have involved satellites, heavy equipment transporters, flying training, search and rescue operations and the future strategic tanker aircraft (FSTA: a replacement for the RAF's air-to-air refuelling aircraft fleet). FSTA involves the UK MoD paying for the availability and use of air tanker capability and services with a leasing contract for services and operational service. It replaced the traditional solution whereby the RAF owned, operated and serviced its fleet of tanker aircraft. This contract is also different in that it involves the provision of a complete military capability (aircraft, spares, maintenance, training of flight crews and other personnel, and some sponsored reserve air and ground crews) which is closer to the front-line than most PFI/PPP contracts. It requires the private contractor to provide capability during peace-time, transition to war and conflict. The partnering element in the contract allows the contractor to hire any spare capacity to third parties (e.g. for commercial air freight operations); but the RAF will always have first call on all the aircraft in an emergency. Overall, this policy involved a complex contractual arrangement and agreement creating substantial transaction costs.

1.18.6 A critique

PFI/PPP agreements are expected to lead to cost savings from competition, innovation and contractual efficiency incentives. The result should be lower construction costs and lower life-cycle costs as risks are transferred to the private sector and contractors are encouraged to be innovative in project design, construction, operation and maintenance. One fallacy must be addressed. Simply transferring resources from the public to the private sector has no effect on efficiency if identical resources are used. A further complication arises since governments can always borrow more cheaply than the private sector (one to three percentage points in the UK): hence, if PFI/PPP is to result in cost savings, the extra financing costs for the private sector must be offset by savings elsewhere over the life-cycle of the project.

Any evaluation of military outsourcing needs to ask *who gains and who loses* from this policy? In theory, taxpayers should gain from 'better value for money' but they might lose if the results are not value for money. Other gainers include private industry, which wins the contracts, banks, which provide the finance, shareholders and lawyers, who advise both government and industry on the legal implications of PFI/PPP contracts. Losers include the public sector workers who lose their jobs or receive lower pay as the 'in-house' unit is taken-over by a private contractor (e.g. replacing full-time workers with part-time workers). The policy can also be a mechanism for intergenerational welfare shifting. The present generation of voters/taxpayers benefits from the assets (e.g. hospitals, roads) but bequeaths to the next generations a run-down public asset base and an extensive network of contractual commitments to buy output from the PFI/PPP assets.

There are also substantial transaction costs involved in writing, enforcing and monitoring long duration contracts which will deliver services of approved quality. Problems arise from uncertainty, which stems from unforeseen and unforeseeable events that are difficult to include in a legally enforceable contract. As a result, long duration contracts require trust, commitment and partnership between both parties. Trust is based on expectations of *future* behaviour and it will be affected by reputation that is based on *past* behaviour and performance. Partnering involves the use of one or a few long-term suppliers based on reputation and trust which replaces competitive contracting. Nonetheless, where there are few contractors, as in defence, there remain risks of collusion and small numbers bargaining.

Once awarded a long-term contract, the successful firm will become a monopoly supplier. A firm will seek to exploit its monopoly power (information advantage: opportunism) and earn monopoly profits (excessive profits). For example, they might economise or default on those parts of the contract which have not been specified completely (e.g. aspects of quality). Here, a possible safeguard for governments is provided by a firm's concern with its reputation and its desire for future government contracts.

In principle, a properly organised PFI/PPP should provide information on the benefits and costs of different levels of provision, embracing both quantity and quality aspects (i.e. marginal benefit/cost calculations). However, questions arise as to whether such an approach is applied to the public sector comparators, whether invitations to tender result in such information and whether contracts allow firms to 'trade-off' quantity against quality?

The standard textbook model regards defence as a pure public good, usually involving both public finance and public provision. In contrast, PFI/PPP shows opportunities for both private finance and private provision of defence activities. The policy is claimed to lead to cost savings, estimated by MoD at some 5% to 40%. However, it is difficult to assess the reliability of such MoD claims: they might involve quality reductions; there is no indication of the cost base to which the savings apply (e.g. 40% saving on £1 million or on £100 million); and the savings cannot be verified until the contracts have been completed, which will be in the 'long-run' (when we are all dead!). For example, over a thirty-year contract, the estimated savings might not be achieved. There is also the problem of the 'counterfactual', namely, what would have happened in the absence of the PFI/PPP contract (e.g. with the activity retained 'in-house')?

Applied to defence activities, PFI/PPP policy raises further problems. There are problems and costs of writing and enforcing long duration contracts (twenty-five to thirty years) which deliver a range of services of approved quality for a range of unknown and unknowable future contingencies, varying from peace to war (with a variety of enemies and threats). With such contracts, industry will always seek to protect itself from income losses (e.g. by seeking cancellation payments or contract renegotiation) even where there is supposed to be 'trust and partnering'. Similarly, government will always be tempted to use its bargaining power to renegotiate a contract, especially where it believes that industry is earning 'excessive profits'. Trust and partnering are attractive concepts, but ones which are difficult to 'operationalise' where the parties to a contract have different objectives.

Furthermore, firms have incentives to economise or default on those parts of the contract which are difficult and costly to specify and enforce; and this behaviour might have serious implications for military capability (i.e. the difference between success and failure in conflict). Once again, a firm's concern for its reputation will act as a constraint on such behaviour.

Uncertainty arises over the willingness of private contractor's staff to serve close to the front-line during conflict. While efforts are made to ensure that 'key personnel' are 'sponsored reserves' (i.e. can be called-up in conflict and are subject to military command), it is not known whether other contractor's staff will be willing to supply their labour in a conflict situation.

Finally, there is the task of formulating contracts which allow competition to achieve both technical and allocative efficiency. Nor should efficiency be regarded as a static concept: competition also encourages innovation. The task for MoD is to formulate its requirements so as to encourage rival bidders to offer alternative and innovatory solutions. For example, a competition for military flying training needs to avoid specifying the minimum number of actual aircraft flying hours, their location and the type of aircraft. Such a specification would exclude the possibility of innovatory solutions such as the use of flight simulators and/or training at overseas locations which might train pilots faster and at lower-cost. Ultimately, the end-output of military flying training is the 'production' of trained pilots (i.e. achieving a certified level of competence).

1.18.7 Future Possibilities

In the UK, there is considerable experience with the use of private contractors in military support operations (i.e. private firms substituted for public 'in-house' units). Nonetheless, the inevitable question concerns the limits of such private sector inputs into military operations. Is there an 'essential core' of military operations that must always be provided by public sector 'in-house' units? Here, two further policy options can be considered, namely, leasing arrangements and private companies undertaking combat missions.

1.18.8 Leasing Arrangements Using Private Finance

Under this option, equipment might be leased from defence firms rather than purchased for ownership by the armed forces. Defence firms would enter into long-term contracts offering to provide a guaranteed number of operationally available front-line equipment units on a daily basis (e.g. combat aircraft, tanks) with the contractor responsible for maintenance and repair for the duration of the contract and eventual disposal of the equipment. Risk assessment would be a major challenge when writing such contracts, with the need to allow for use, destruction and replacement in both peace and conflict (currently, the armed forces bear such risks). Also, such options would need a thorough evaluation of the benefits and costs of leasing versus an outright purchase, where the purchase option requires the armed forces to assume the responsibility for maintenance, repair and replacement of equipment. Recently, both the UK and USA have introduced leasing arrangements for the purchase of transport and tanker air-craft. However, US studies have shown that the benefits of leasing compared with purchasing are sensitive to the financing assumptions and that any analysis by the armed forces needs to be subjected to critical scrutiny (CBO, 2003).

1.18.9 Private Companies Providing Combat Missions

This is an area in which there is little published information. Obvious examples include the use of mercenaries in countries such as Africa (e.g. Sandline company). As with the leasing option, a key issue concerns the costs of under-taking transactions (i.e. of doing business/of contracting: remembering that all modes of organisation are flawed). Consider some of the issues that are likely to arise if private firms were to be involved in combat roles.

i) Unforeseen contingencies. There are problems of writing and enforcing contracts for unforeseen contingencies and various threats where uncer-tainty dominates. For example, a contract might require the capture of a town held by rebels, but this becomes more complicated if other nations were to later enter the conflict in support of the rebels so changing the contract requirements. Problems arise because firms do not know the resources required to complete the contract. A typical solution to such uncertainty is to write a cost-plus contract or a target cost incentive fee contract but such contracts change efficiency incentives and transfer risks from the contractor to the state.

ii) Asset specificity. Some equipment and training has little value in alterna-tive civilian uses so that firms will be unwilling to invest considerable resources in acquiring such assets (hold-up problem).

iii) Loyalty, trust and reputation. Heads of state need to be confident of the loyalty of their armed forces. There is a belief that national (public) military forces are more likely to be loyal and trustworthy than private companies. Moreover, private companies can withdraw from combat contracts or they can change sides (although it is not unknown for national (public) armed forces to mutiny, retreat and surrender). However, firms that default on combat contracts would suffer reputation effects (however, this does not help the nation left with the task of protecting its citizens).

iv) Unpredicted and adverse results. Contracts and performance indicators for private firms can give unexpected and undesirable results. For example, private firms seeking to minimise costs might impose collateral damage and costs on civilians, they might avoid losing their costly assets, reducing effectiveness, or they might deliberately prolong the conflict in order to extend or expand their monetary gains.

Undoubtedly, the use of private firms in combat roles is controversial.[11] The benefits and costs of such private roles need to be identified and critically evaluated (including identifying the myths, emotion and special pleading which exist in this area). At the minimum, consideration of private companies providing combat missions will identify the limits of private sector inputs into military operations. It might also identify new opportunities for using private contractors either in the armed forces or in support of the armed forces. Examples include the use of private contractors in peacekeeping zones for training, security guarding and policing roles, so releasing military forces for use in combat missions (Fredland and Kendry, 1999; HCP 577, 2002).

1.18.10 Conclusion on Military Outsourcing

With regard to defence activities, two broad policy alternatives are available, namely, 'in-house' versus outsourcing, both raise questions about the boundaries of government activities in defence. Why do governments contract-out some activities and undertake others 'in-house'? The broad trade-offs can be identified. Private firms offer high-powered efficiency incentives but there are the costs of contracting under uncertainty (i.e. negotiating, agreeing, policing and enforcing). In contrast, public agencies offer only low-powered efficiency incentives, but they are good on loyalty and trust, which are attributes provided by national military forces.

Public sector 'in-house' solutions do not solve the problems of public monopoly (i.e. inefficiency, poor quality and lack of innovation). They involve long-term contracts (in perpetuity) with a public monopoly and no re-contracting. Efficient private sector solutions require market competition or contestability, but with long-term contracts, such rivalry is confined to the initial award stage. Also, private sector solutions in such forms as PFI/PPPs involve substantial transaction costs. In defence, PFI/PPPs involve long-term contracts that are characterised by incompleteness in their specification, asset specificity and scope for opportunism because of asymmetric information. As a result, the alternative forms of provision need to be assessed critically and evaluated with evidence on their benefits and costs. What are the estimated cost savings from private sector inputs into military operations? Are such estimated savings achieved? What are the impacts on quality? Also, those set to gain and lose

---

[11] Machiavelli had clear views on mercenary forces. They were regarded as 'both useless and dangerous: disunited, ambitious and without discipline and in war they will either run away or march off. Also, they devised rules of war aimed to avoid exposing themselves and their men to great fatigue and danger' (Machiavelli, 2004, pp. 63–64, 69). Further, he concluded that a wise Prince should rely exclusively on his own troops composed of 'his own subjects or citizens' (Machiavelli, 2004, p. 74).

need to be identified. Who gains and who loses from the changes (e.g. tax-payers, firms, shareholders, military personnel, lawyers and financial institutions)? As shown above, defence economics has achieved much but major challenges remain.

2 Challenges

While much has been achieved in establishing defence economics as a reputable part of mainstream economics, numerous challenges remain. There are major research gaps including the valuation of defence output, data availability, studies of the world's defence industries, assessing the causes and impact of rising costs, and career opportunities for young defence economists. But defence economics has not remained static: it has adjusted to new threats, new theories and new estimating techniques.

2.1 New Developments

2.1.1 Terrorism

New military threats have been addressed by defence and peace economists. Terrorism is an obvious example with the most high profile recent example being the 9/11 terror attacks on the USA. The standard response was that terrorism is not a subject for defence economists and should be left to other social science disciplines (e.g. political science, sociology, international relations and strategic studies). On the contrary, defence economists showed that their discipline could make a valuable contribution to understanding terrorism and policy solutions. A pioneer in the field is Todd Sandler (2018).

A starting point showing the contribution of economics is provided by a simple economics description of the 9/11 attacks. The September 11, 2001, attacks on the World Trade Center and the Pentagon showed how terrorists created a small air force using captured airliners as flying bombs with personnel committed to suicide attacks. This small but deadly air force was cheap to create (c.f. the large size and costs of the USAF) without a costly equipment acquisition programme and maintenance infrastructure. The terrorists simply stole the airliners. The result was almost 3,000 deaths and estimated economic losses of US$80–90 billion (2005 prices (Barros et al., 2005)).

Terrorism is analysed applying choice theoretic and game theory models. Choice theoretic models apply standard consumer choice theory. Terrorists are assumed to maximise a utility function subject to budget constraints represented by a given income and by the relative prices of various goods. The utility function can show choices between attack methods, such as skyjackings and bombings, or between the alternatives of terrorist and peaceful activities. Within the model, substitution effects offer powerful insights showing that public policies that increase the relative price of one attack method, such as sky-jackings, will encourage terrorists to substitute an alternative and lower-cost attack method, such as assassinations, bombings, kidnappings and hostage-taking. There are also collective action problems where nations have incentives to 'free ride' on any nation that introduces 'strong' action against international terrorists. For example, many nations chose to free ride and avoided contributing to the US invasion of Afghanistan and Iraq designed to increase the costs of terrorism.

Terrorism involves game theory through strategic interactions between terrorist groups and governments. Terrorists respond to enhanced government security measures by changing their tactics, targets and locations of attacks. In response, governments change their behaviour to impede terrorism by restricting access to funds and supporters, through attacks on their bases and training areas, and by increasing security against specific forms of attack. For example, the hijacking and bombing of airliners has been made more difficult through greater airport security. But counter-terrorism measures are costly in both monetary and non-monetary terms. Increased airport security involves greater time spent by airliner passengers in queues awaiting screening (a non-monetary cost (Sandler, 2018; Sandler and Hartley, 2003)).

Terrorist groups are also much more complex than a single individual and should be analysed as households and firms. Often, the terrorist household forms a firm capable of training terrorists and manufacturing small arms for the group (e.g. planning and reconnaissance, suicide vests and improvised explosive devices). Terrorists and rebel groups form violent non-state actors that are independent of nation states and which use violence to achieve their objectives where there are challenges in modelling their armament choices.

2.1.2 New Military Technology

Military technology involves the application of new ideas to military products and capabilities used by the armed forces as well as the application of new ideas to defence industry production processes. Examples include the use of drones and space systems by the armed forces and the application of artificial intelligence, robotics and supercomputing in the research, development and production phases in defence industries.

Historically, there are numerous examples of new military technology affecting the armed forces and defence industries. Rifles replaced bows and arrows, cannons destroyed castles, metal warships with steam engines replaced wooden vessels powered by sail, drones replaced manned aircraft and space satellites revolutionised communications (replacing pigeons, balloons and radios). Even more dramatic was the impact of the aeroplane which led to a new armed force (air forces), a new weapon of war (aircraft and their use as fighters and bombers) and a new industry, namely, the aircraft industry. Military aircraft also developed into civil transports often applying some military technologies to airliners (e.g. technology spin-offs such as aero-engines, radar and avionics).

New military technology is costly. Augustine forecast rising unit costs in real terms and the long-run prospect of a single tank army, single ship navy and *Starship Enterprise* for the air force! This suggests a new class of defence equipment known as Augustine goods. These are viewed as a cost-effective means of securing peace. They are in contrast with views of today's battlefield focused on large numbers of small, cheap, expendable and autonomous systems (Brauer et al., 2020).

New military technology means new threats to which the armed forces have to respond. Threats are uncertain and sometimes unknown and unknowable and they originate from nation states and terrorist groups. New threats require a response from the armed forces and defence industries, which supply new equipment to meet the changing demands of the military forces. New military technology means new market opportunities for defence industries providing incentives for mergers, acquisitions and the creation of new divisions within companies (involving start-up costs). In some cases, new technology might emerge from industries outside of defence leading to 'spin-ins'. Examples include IT, computers, mobile phones and space satellites.

New military technology might result in a revolution in military affairs. There will be new opportunities for substitution and the end of some of the traditional monopoly property rights of each of the armed forces. For example, manned combat aircraft operated by the air force might replace army soldiers, attack helicopters operated by the army might replace close air support aircraft operated by the air force, anti-submarine maritime patrol aircraft operated by the air force might replace frigates operated by the navy, air force land-based aircraft might replace naval aircraft carriers and surface-to-air missiles operated by the army might replace manned fighter aircraft operated by the air force. Overall, new military technology might lead to new equipment replacing military and civilian personnel. More generally, new military technology raises questions about future equipment unit costs and whether the result is a greater likelihood of war or peace.

2.1.3 Disarmament

The end of the Cold War and the super power arms race between the USA and the Soviet Union meant reduced defence spending resulting in disarmament and the prospect of a peace dividend. Disarmament became the focus of defence economists and they contributed to knowledge of the process by stressing that disarmament resembled an investment process involving short run costs for long-run benefits. Disarmament is an adjustment process and the task of re-allocating resources from the defence economy to the civilian sector takes time and involves costs: we do not live in a world of magic wand economics where resources are instantly and costlessly shifted from defence to civil activities. Instead, adjustment costs take the form of unemployment and under-employment of resources of labour, capital and land affecting both the armed forces and defence industries. Short run costs eventually lead to long-run benefits in the form of peace and a peace dividend reflected in a greater output of civil goods and services (Hartley and Sandler, 2001; UNIDIR, 1993).

2.1.4 War

The end of the Cold War did not mean a long-lasting peace. Instead, there were wars and conflicts in Europe, Africa and the Middle East. Examples included the Yugoslav Wars as well as Afghanistan, Iraq, Israel, Syria and Yemen. While conflict involves a variety of disciplines and moral and legal judgements, there is also a role for defence and peace economists. Wars are costly (e.g. the Second World War): they destroy economic infrastructure (houses, factories, bridges); and lead to deaths and injuries for military and civilian personnel with military occupation resulting in slavery and starvation (e.g. occupied Europe in the Second World War). Economists contribute further to understanding the causes of conflicts as well as advising on target selection. The Second World War examples included target selection for the allied strategic bombing of Germany, including aircraft and ball bearing factories, submarine yards, dams and oil fields. More recently, economists have addressed newer developments in conflict, embracing genocide, ethnic cleansing and civil wars as well as solutions through international collective action as demonstrated by international peacekeeping forces (Anderton and Carter, 2019; Braddon and Hartley, 2011; Sandler and Hartley, 2003).

Estimates are available for the costs of recent wars. The US budgetary costs of its wars in the Middle East over the period 2001–18 totalled US$5.9 trillion and the US costs of its war in Afghanistan totalled some US$2 trillion by late 2019 (Crawford, 2018). A 2008 study, estimated that the true cost of the Iraq war to the US economy would exceed US$3 trillion. This figure should be compared with the government's initial estimates of US$50 billion (Stiglitz and Bilmes, 2008). Estimating war costs is fraught with difficulties arising from identifying all economic costs and then placing a value on them.

For example, reporting government budgetary costs is only a starting point. Deaths and injuries to military personnel need to be included with valuations placed on losses of life and injuries. Similarly, losses of military equipment need to be identified with valuations placed on such military capital, some of which might be no longer produced. Furthermore, there are costs for the Iraq economy and population and for the USA's allies (e.g. Australia, Poland and the UK).

Economic models start by viewing wars as the use of military force to achieve a re-allocation of resources within and between nations. Nations invade other nations to capture or steal their resources (e.g. land, minerals, oil, water and populations). Wars and conflict destroy markets, and physical and human capital (deaths and injuries) leading to disequilibrium and chaos. Military occupation of a country also involves policing and enforcement costs: occupied populations and slave labour are not willing and voluntary suppliers of labour and will fail to supply labour effort efficiently. All of which further complicates the task of estimating the costs of conflict. Valuing ammunition used and weapons destroyed form only a part of war costs. Further costs arise in valuing lives lost and injuries and then there are the costs of slavery and the valuations placed on losses of freedoms, movement and liberties. Such costings contribute to the challenging task of valuing defence output.

2.2 Defence Output

Defence provides an output in the form of security comprising peace, protection, economic stability, individual and national freedoms, liberty and a national way of life. It also contributes to prosperity through protection from external attack, which provides the conditions allowing beneficial trade and exchange within an economy. Protection of international trade routes further enhances prosperity by promoting the conditions for international trade and exchange between economies. Defence output can also be viewed as providing a stream of benefits, both economic and non-economic. Economic benefits are those defence outputs that contribute to national welfare or GDP. The non-economic benefits of defence include foreign policy benefits, contributions to peacekeeping, peacemaking and disaster relief as well as a nation's prestige and its 'feel good factor'. These defence outputs are difficult to measure and value in monetary form and the problems are increased by the public goods features of defence (Hartley, 2015).

Defence economists rarely address the task of defining and valuing defence output; they usually make vague references to peace, protection and security. Traditionally, government statisticians and the national accounts have measured defence output on the input–output basis, assuming that inputs equal outputs. This convention applied to all public sector activities, including state-provided education, health and roads; where these goods and services are privately provided, they produce market-valued outputs. Improving on the limited inputs equal outputs approach to measuring defence output requires more analysis and evaluation of the basic concept of defence output.

Starting from basic principles suggests various views about the meaning of defence output. In addition to the features outlined above, defence output can be viewed in terms of threats and risks and the contribution of defence to risk avoidance and risk reduction. The risk approach suggests defence as an insurance in response to various current and future known and unknown threats and contingencies. Or, defence can be viewed as providing protection and saving lives, which raises questions about the valuation of life. In addition to saving lives, successful defence protection in the form of avoiding conflict also avoids damage and destruction of property and infrastructure (human and physical capital saved). Furthermore, defence might prevent the foreign military occupation of a country where such occupation might lead to a slave economy. Military occupation could mean the loss of freedoms and starvation (e.g. Nazi Germany's occupation of Europe in the Second World War).

Another approach to measuring defence output focuses on its economic benefits. These are extensive and include its contribution to national and international prosperity, the avoidance of conflict and the cost savings from peace as well as the contribution of armed forces and national defence industries to jobs, technology, spin-offs, exports and import-savings. Such economic benefits of defence need to be assessed critically. Economists focus on the alternative-use value of resources used by the armed forces and defence industries. Would the resources employed by the armed forces and defence industries make a greater contribution to jobs, technology and the balance of payments if used elsewhere in the economy? Critics of the alternative-use question demand that economists specify where these resources would be employed. The answer is that there are a range of alternative industries, such as motor cars, pharmaceuticals and alternative energy uses (e.g. green industries). In the last resort, markets determine the alternative uses for resources, depending on how well and quickly labour and capital markets work (market failures can be corrected by governments through, say, labour market policies such as grants for training and mobility).

Some nations have moved from the traditional input equals output approach to measuring defence output. One solution is to define defence output in terms of military capabilities, such as the capability of deploying, say, an infantry brigade with air and sea support to the Middle East or Far East for various time periods (e.g. a few weeks; six months, a year or indefinitely). Deploying an infantry brigade of, say, 5,000 personnel overseas for a substantial period is labour-intensive. For example, a deployment of 5,000 personnel for six months with returns every two years might require a multiple of at least five times the basic deployment, namely, some 25,000 personnel. While a focus on military capability is an improvement on the traditional input equals outputs approach, there is still an absence of any money valuations of the capabilities.

Future research to identify and value defence output might explore opportunities for using approaches based on value of life studies and by considering defence as an insurance good. The experience of health economists in developing and using QALYS (quality-adjusted life years) might lead to the emergence of PALYS or protection-adjusted life years. But developing measures of defence output and valuing them will be a major research effort requiring considerable time and resources. Is there a research framework capable of providing the required research effort?

2.3 Future Researchers

Defence economics lacks an adequate human capital research base, especially of young researchers with the incentives and resources to challenge conventional wisdom. Employment opportunities for young defence economics researchers are limited. Obvious employment opportunities exist in government defence ministries and other government departments (e.g. treasury, trade and industry), in universities, in 'think tanks' and in defence companies. However, many of these organisations have limited staff and are often motivated by the need to focus on immediate policy-relevant research questions. For example, what are the employment impacts of buying British military equipment? Questions of basic research, such as developing measures of defence output, are regarded as too long-term with no prospects of useable results in the near term. Potentially, university researchers are the obvious focus for addressing basic research questions in defence economics. But the field has failed to attract young defence economics researchers, which reflects the preponderance of incentives in university research: career prospects are in mainstream areas (e.g. macroeconomics, financial economics and general equilibrium) and not in defence and peace economics. This position is reinforced by a lack of funds for PhD students in the field and a lack of defence economics lectureships.

The availability of reliable data for defence economics research encounters similar problems. Research organisations such as SIPRI appear to have 'solved' this problem by raising funds for the collection and publication of reliable data in the field of defence and peace economics. Examples include data on world military expenditure, the top 100 arms companies and the international arms trade. SIPRI is successful because it offers its researchers income and career prospects. Nonetheless, SIPRI is not immune from funding problems and still has to raise the necessary funds.

2.4 The Impact of Rising Costs

Military equipment has two cost dimensions: it is costly and unit costs continue to rise. Measuring and explaining these cost trends is important research. Technical progress is one possible cause of rising costs: new military equipment is costlier and without similar increases in defence budgets, numbers of front-line equipment will decline. New technology will also lead to radical changes in the future battlefield with future prospects of battlefields with large numbers of drones, robot soldiers and spaceships. New technology will mean a different future and one where defence economics will still have a contribution to make: new weapons systems will be costly and not immune from the defence economics problem.

2.5 Other Research Opportunities

New research opportunities remain. There are opportunities for research into the world's defence industries, especially those countries which are less well known such as Iran, Pakistan, Saudi Arabia and those in the nations of south and central America and Africa (Hartley and Belin, 2020). Further research work is needed into the defence economies of specific nations, using a standard format so enabling comparisons between countries (see country surveys in *Defence and Peace Economics*). Each country survey would review basic data on its defence sector (e.g. defence spending, armed forces and defence industries) and review their future prospects.

Other areas offer research prospects. Two examples include case studies of major arms projects and major arms firms. Some nations (e.g. the USA and UK) have a considerable literature on their major arms procurements, such as the acquisition of aircraft carriers, modern combat aircraft and missiles. These provide the basis for in-depth case studies reviewing the success and failure of projects, reflected in cost overruns and delays. A similar case study approach can be applied to major arms firms. Examples include Airbus, BAE Systems, Boeing and Lockheed Martin whose annual reports provide a valuable research tool with data on sales, employment and profitability. Here, problems arise where company annual reports do not separate defence from civil business providing only totals for all their business.

Opportunities exist for further research into the international arms trade, especially the trade in small arms and illegal arms trading (e.g. what is known about international arms dealers?). Terrorist groups are also involved in the international arms trade: what is known, what is not known and what needs to be known about their role in these markets? Corruption is a further characteristic of arms dealing: an area where little is known and some light needs to be shed on this topic.

The availability of reliable data remains a problem for defence economics researchers. Nonetheless, there is more out there than originally expected.[12] Some areas have insurmountable barriers. Secrecy dominates some fields, such as research into nuclear, chemical and biological warfare. Even democracies have their 'black' programmes (US research into stealth aircraft).

2.6 Conclusion

Much has been achieved. There is now a greater understanding of the contribution of economics to the studies of war and peace. The range of topics that have been addressed is impressive. New models have been developed of the arms race, the demand for military expenditure, growth, prosperity and defence spending. Further topics include military alliances, equipment procurement, armed forces personnel, defence industries, the arms trade, disarmament and conversion. Nor has the field remained static. Models have emerged to deal with completely new issues such as terrorism, civil wars, revolutions, genocide and ethnic cleansing.

Defence economics has embraced many of the advances in theoretical and empirical economics. Game theory has been applied widely to such topics as arms races, military alliances, procurement, terrorism and conflict. Public economics has benefited from the analysis of public goods, free riding and collective action problems (e.g. United Nations peacekeeping). Further developments involving the application of public choice analysis and principal-agent models have increased our understanding of procurement policy.

The latest empirical techniques have been applied. Time-series tools have been applied to the study of growth and military spending, arms races and terrorism. Tools used include Granger causality, cointegration tests and vector autoregressions (VAR). Following a large empirical literature on Granger causality tests for the relationship between military spending and the economy, a critical review concluded '... that Granger causality test statistics are

---

[12] I am reminded of my early days working as a PhD student on the economics of the UK aircraft industry. A visiting professor with experience of the industry once told me that there was not a PhD on the aircraft industry. Later, I obtained my doctorate on the industry, developed my interests into the wider defence economics field and am still writing about the industry.

uninformative about the size or direction of the predicted effects' and do not measure economic causality (Dunne and Smith, 2010, p. 440).

History cannot be ignored, especially the Second World War and the Vietnam War. The Second World War saw applications of economics to battlefield choices. Economics and operations analysis were used in target selection and assessment for the strategic bombing offensive against Germany. The USA selected economic targets for its bomber offensive, such as oil fields, aircraft and ball bearing factories, submarine yards and transport facilities. The results showed the limitations of economics with factories being dispersed and relocated, damaged factories repaired quickly and alternative suppliers emerging (i.e. a failure to recognise how economies adjust to major shocks). The notion of a 'vital' industry was exposed and often the costs of destroying such targets was found to be considerable (e.g. air raids on the ball bearing factories at Schweinfurt).

Similarly, economics was used in the Vietnam War with the application of programme budgeting and cost-effectiveness analysis. Input–output relationships were found to be simplistic and misleading. For example, the relationship between numbers of bombs dropped and enemy casualties led US defence staffs to conclude that the enemy was destroyed; but they kept reappearing!

Defence economics has influenced policy. A classic example was the estimation of the costs of war, especially the US costs of conflicts in Afghanistan and Iraq and the differences between initial low estimates and the final massive costs of these conflicts (Stiglitz and Bilmes, 2008). Defence economics has also influenced military thinking and armed forces personnel are now much more familiar with economic concepts, such as budget constraints, opportunity costs and the need to make choices. Economists are also employed in national defence departments.

What does the future hold for defence economics? Much of the discipline developed against the background of the Cold War with its arms race, deterrence and clear fixed threats involving the former Soviet Union and the USA. Now the world is different with 'unknown unknowns' and defence economists needing to think outside the traditional optimising-equilibrium models. Military power may no longer be the sole focus for studying defence, peace and security. Instead, a focus on national security might identify a range of alternative policy options outside of national military power. Examples include national police forces, the notion of acceptable risk, the role of international collective action, economic sanctions and foreign aid. The international security situation is also changing with the emergence of new military powers such as China, Iran and North Korea capable of challenging US military power with the prospect of the USA as a declining world power (McGuire, 2010).

Defence economics remains a relatively under-researched field. There are plenty of opportunities for young thrusting researchers. This Element has identified some of these research opportunities. Developing human capital in the field requires mentors and funders able to provide a research environment that encourages and rewards the study of defence economics.

References

Anderton, C. H. and Carter, J. R. (2007). A survey of peace economics. In T. Sandler and K. Hartley, eds., *Handbook of Defense Economics*, 1211–1258, vol 2, Amsterdam: North Holland.

Arena, M., Younossi. O., Brancato, K., Blickstun, I. and Grunmich, C. A. (2008). *Why Has the Cost of Fixed Wing Aircraft Risen?*, Santa Monica, CA: Rand.

Asher, H. (1956). *Cost-Quantity Relationships in the Airframe Industry*, Santa Monica, CA: Rand.

Anderton, C. H. and Carter, J. R. (2019). *Principles of Conflict Economics*, Cambridge: Cambridge University Press.

Barros, C. P., Kollias, C. and Sandler, T. (2005). Security challenges and threats in a post-9/11 world. *Defence and Peace Economics*, **16**(6), 1–3.

Benoit, E. (1973). *Defense and Economic Growth in Developing Countries*, Boston, MA: Lexington Books.

Bicksler, B. A., Gilroy, C. L. and Warner, J. T., eds. (2004). *The All-Volunteer Force: Thirty Years of Service*, Washington, DC: Brasseys.

Braddon, D. L. and Hartley, K., eds. (2011). *Handbook on the Economics of Conflict*, Cheltenham: Edward Elgar.

Brauer, J. and Van Tuyll, H. (2008). *Castles, Battles and Bombs*, Chicago, IL: University of Chicago Press.

Brauer, J., Hartley, K. and Markowski, S. (2020). Rethinking Augustine's Law: armament costs and evolving military technology. In G. Partha, ed., *Essays in Honour of Manas Chatterji*, Bingley: Emerald.

Cmnd 3223 (1996). *Statement on the Defence Estimates 1996*, London: HMSO.

COW (2020). The Correlates of War Project website, correlatesofwar.org/.

CBO (2020). *The Costs of Replacing the Department of Defense's Current Aviation Fleet*, February, Washington, DC: Congressional Budget Office.

Crawford, N. C. (2018). *The Costs of War*, Providence, Rhode Island: Watson Institute, Brown University.

Davies, N. Eager, A., Maier, M. and Penfold, L. (2011). *Intergenerational Equipment Cost Escalation*, Defence Economics Research Paper, London: Ministry of Defence.

Deger, S. and Smith, R.P. (1983). Military expenditure and growth in less developed countries. *Journal of Conflict Resolution*, **27**(2), 335–53.

DoD (2019). *National Defense Budget Estimates for FY 2020*, Washington, DC: Department of Defense.

Dunne, P and Smith, R. P. (2010). Military expenditure and Granger causality: a critical review, *Defence and Peace Economics*, **21**(5–6), 427–41.

Downs, A. (1957). *An Economic Theory of Democracy*, New York: Harper and Row.

d'Agostino, G., Dunne, J. P. and Pieroni, L. (2019). Military expenditure, endogeneity and economic growth. *Defence and Peace Economics*, **30**(5), 509–24.

EDA (2018). *Defence Data 2017–18*, Brussels: European Defence Agency.

Fredland, E. and Kendry, A. (1999). The privatisation of military force. *Cambridge Review of International Affairs*, **XIII**(1), 147–64.

Gaffney, D. and Pollock, A. M. (1999). Pump-priming the PFI. *Public Money and Management*, **19**(1), 55–62.

Gates, T. S. (1970). *Report of the President's Commission on an All-Volunteer Force*, Washington, DC: US Government Printing Office.

Hartley, K. (2011). *The Economics of Defence Policy: A New Perspective*, Abingdon: Routledge.

Hartley, K. (2014). *The Political Economy of Aerospace Industries*, Cheltenham: Edward Elgar.

Hartley, K. (2015). Measuring defence output. In F. Melese, A. Richter and B. Solomon, eds., *Military Cost–Benefit Analysis*, London: Routledge.

Hartley, K. (2018a). Defence budgets. In D. J. Galbreath and J. R. Deni, eds., *Routledge Handbook of Defence Studies*, Abingdon: Routledge.

Hartley, K. (2018b). The profitability of non-competitive defence contracts: the UK experience. *Defence and Peace Economics*, **29**(6), 577–94.

Hartley, K. (2019). The political economy of arms collaboration. In R. Matthews, ed., *The Political Economy of Defence*, Cambridge: Cambridge University Press.

Hartley, K. (2020). Rising costs – Augustine revisited. *Defence and Peace Economics*, Thirtieth Anniversary Issue, 434–442, vol 31, 4.

Hartley, K. and Belin, J. (2020). *The Economics of the Global Defence Industry*, Abingdon: Routledge.

Hartley, K. and Sandler, T., eds. (2001). *The Economics of Defence*, vols 1–3, The International Library of Critical Writings in Economics 128, Cheltenham: Elgar.

Hartley, K. and Solomon, B. (2016). Defence inflation: multi-country perspectives and prospects. *Defence and Peace Economics*, **27**(2), 161–298.

Hitch, C. J. and McKean, R. (1960). *The Economics of Defense in the Nuclear Age*, Cambridge, MA: Harvard University Press.

HCP 577 (2002). *Private Military Companies: Options for Regulation*, London: Foreign and Commonwealth Office, The Stationery Office.

IEP (2019a). *Global Terrorism Index 2019*, Sydney: Institute for Economics and Peace.

IEP (2019b). *Global Peace Index 2019*, Sydney: Institute for Economics and Peace.

IISS (2019). *The Military Balance 2019*, London: International Institute for Strategic Studies.

Isard, W. (1994). Peace economics: a topical perspective. *Peace Economics, Peace Science and Public Policy*, 1, 9–11.

ITERATE (2019). *International Terrorism: Attributes of Terrorist Events*, Micklous, E. F., Sandler, T., Murdock, J. M. and Fleming, P. A., Harvard, MA: Harvard University, Numeric Data Services Dataverse.

Jackson, P. M. (1982). *The Political Economy of Bureaucracy*, Oxford: Philip Allan.

Kirkpatrick, D. (2019). The whole-life costs of defence equipment. In R. Matthews, ed., *The Political Economy of Defence*, 283–306, Cambridge: Cambridge University Press.

Kirkpatrick, D. and Pugh. P. (1983). Towards the Starship Enterprise – Are the Current Trends in Unit Costs Inexorable? Aerospace 16–23, May, London.

Machiavelli, N. (2004). *The Prince and the Art of War*, London: Collector's Library.

Matthews, R., ed. (2019). *The Political Economy of Defence*, Cambridge: Cambridge University Press.

McGuire, M. (2010). Agenda for defence and peace economics. *Defence and Peace Economics*, **21**(5–6), 529–34.

Middleton, A., Bowns, S., Hartley, K. and Reid, J. (2006). The effect of defence R&D on military equipment quality. *Defence and Peace Economics*, **17**(2), 117–39.

Mill, J. S. (1883). *Principles of Political Economy*, London: Longmans, Green and Co.

MoD (2017). *Defence Inflation Estimates 2015/16*, Finance and Economics Annual Bulletin, January, London: Ministry of Defence.

Mueller, D. C. (1989). *Public Choice II: A revised edition of Public Choice*, Cambridge: Cambridge University Press.

NATO (2019). *Defence Expenditure of NATO Countries*, Brussels: *NATO*.

Oi, W. Y. (1967). The economic cost of the draft. *American Economic Review*, **57**(2), 59–62.

Olson, M. (1965). *The Logic of Collective Action*, Cambridge, MA: Harvard University Press.

Olson, M. and Zeckhauser, R. (1966). An economic theory of alliances. *Review of Economics and Statistics*, **48**(3), 266–79.

Parker, D. and Hartley, K. (2003). Transaction costs, relational contracting and public private partnerships: a case study of UK defence. *Journal of Purchasing and Supply Management*, 9, 97–108.

Peck, M. J. and Scherer, F. M. (1962). *The Weapons Acquisition Process: An Economic Analysis*, Boston, MA: Harvard University Press.

Pugh, P. G. (2007). *Source Book of Defence Equipment Costs*, London: Dandy Booksellers.

Rich, M., Stanley, W., Birkler, J. and Hesse, M. (1981). *Multi-National Co-production of Military Aerospace Systems*, Santa Monica, CA; Rand.

Richardson, L. F. (1960). *Arms and Insecurity: A Mathematical Study of the Causes and Origins of War*, Pittsburgh, PA: Homewood.

Rand (2018). *F-35 Block Buy*, Santa Monica, CA: Rand.

Sandler, T. (1992). *Collective Action: Theory and Applications*, Ann Arbour, MI: University of Michigan Press.

Sandler, T. (2018). *Terrorism: What Everyone Needs to Know*, Oxford: Oxford University Press.

Sandler, T. and Hartley, K. (1995). *The Economics of Defense*, Cambridge: Cambridge University Press.

Sandler, T. and Hartley, K., eds. (2003). *The Economics of Conflict*, vols 1–3. The International Library of Critical Writings in Economics 168. Cheltenham: Elgar.

Sandler, T. and Hartley, K., Eds, (2007). *Handbook of Defense Economics, Volume 2, Defense in a Globalized World*, Amsterdam: North Holland.

Scherer, F. M. (1964). *The Weapons Acquisition Process: Economic Incentives*, Boston, MA: Harvard University Press.

Smith, A. (1776). *An Inquiry into the Nature and Causes of the Wealth of Nations*, London: Knight.

Stiglitz, J. and Bilmes, L. (2008). *The Three Trillion Dollar War: The True Costs of the Iraq Conflict*, London: Penguin.

SIPRI (2018). *SIPRI Yearbook: Armaments, Disarmament and International Security*, Oxford: Stockholm International Peace Research Institute, Oxford University Press.

SIPRI (2019). *Military Expenditure Database and Arms Transfer Database*, Stockholm: Stockholm International Peace Research Institute.

SIPRI (2020). *New SIPRI Data Reveals Scale of Chinese Arms Industry*, Stockholm: Stockholm International Peace Research Institute.

Tisdell, C. and Hartley, K. (2008). *Microeconomic Policy: A New Perspective*, Cheltenham: Edward Elgar.

TI (2011). *The Transparency of National Defence Budgets*, London: Transparency International.

Trunkey, R. D. (2019). Operating costs of aging air force aircraft: adjusting for aggregate budget effects. *Defence and Peace Economics*, **30**(4), 454–61.

UNIDIR (1993). *Economic Aspects of Disarmament: Disarmament as an Investment Process*, Geneva: United Nations Institute for Disarmament Research.

Acknowledgement

This Element was reviewed by two anonymous referees. My thanks for their valuable comments. The usual disclaimers apply.

Cambridge Elements ⹀

Defence Economics

Keith Hartley

University of York

Keith Hartley was Professor of Economics and Director of the Centre for Defence Economics at the University of York, where he is now Emeritus Professor of Economics. He is the author of over 500 publications comprising journal articles, books and reports. His most recent books include The Economics of Arms (Agenda Publishing, 2017) and with Jean Belin (Eds) The Economics of the Global Defence Industry (Taylor and Francis, 2020). Hartley was founding Editor of the journal *Defence and Peace Economics*; a NATO Research Fellow; a QinetiQ Visiting Fellow; consultant to the UN, EC, EDA, UK MoD, HM Treasury, Trade and Industry, Business, Innovation and Skills and International Development and previously Special Adviser to the House of Commons Defence Committee.

About the Series

Defence Economics is a relatively new field within the discipline of economics. It studies all aspects of the economics of war and peace. It embraces a wide range of topics in both macroeconomics and microeconomics. Cambridge Elements in Defence Economics aims to publish original and authoritative papers in the field. These will include expert surveys of the foundations of the discipline, its historical development and contributions developing new and novel topics. They will be valuable contributions to both research and teaching in universities and colleges, and will also appeal to other specialist groups comprising politicians, military and industrial personnel as well as informed general readers.

Cambridge Elements ☰

Defence Economics

Elements in the Series

Defence Economics: Achievements and Challenges
Keith Hartley